# THE
# SECRETS TO
# HAPPINESS
# WORK
AT

## HOW TO CHOOSE AND CREATE
## PURPOSE AND FULFILLMENT
## IN YOUR WORK

# TRACY BROWER, PhD

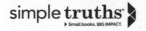

simple **truths**
▶ Small books. BIG IMPACT.

Copyright © 2021, 2024 by Tracy Brower, PhD
Cover and internal design © 2024 by Sourcebooks
Cover design by theBookDesigners
Cover image © GDSign Gusmanfahmi/Shutterstock

This publication is designed to provide accurate and authoritative information
in regard to the subject matter covered. It is sold with the understanding
that the publisher is not engaged in rendering legal, accounting, or other
professional service. If legal advice or other expert assistance is required,
the services of a competent professional person should be sought.—*From
a Declaration of Principles Jointly Adopted by a Committee of the American
Bar Association and a Committee of Publishers and Associations*

Published by Simple Truths, an imprint of Sourcebooks
P.O. Box 4410, Naperville, Illinois 60567–4410
(630) 961-3900
sourcebooks.com

Originally published in 2021 in the United States of America by Sourcebooks.

Cataloging-in-Publication Data is on file with the Library of Congress.

Printed and bound in the United States of America.
VP 10 9 8 7 6 5 4 3 2 1

*For my family—my secret to happiness!*

# CONTENTS

# INTRODUCTION

Happiness at work may seem elusive or out of reach at the moment because—let's face it—things have been tough. But there is hope. Lots of it, in fact.

The last few years have encompassed one of the most significant reinventions of work in history—and likely in our lifetimes. The landscape of work has changed significantly with new options for where, when, and how work happens. But perhaps even more important, people are thinking more consciously than ever about why they work, with whom they work, and for whom they work. People are demanding more from their work experience, more from their employers, and more from their coworkers.

Because work is so central, these shifts mean a lot for our lives and how we live them, including how we spend our time, what we prioritize, and how we derive meaning, fulfillment, and joy.

We have the opportunity for new ideas and insights. If the size of a transformation is associated with the amount of new learning it can generate, surely our brilliance will be magnified manifold as we emerge and embrace this new topography for how we make sense of work as a part of life.

Classic wisdom suggests, "Find a job you love, and you'll never work a day in your life." For many, this may sound too good to be true. After all, work is…well…work. It is often thought of as drudgery—as something that must be done to pay the mortgage, put food on the table, and pay for the other things in life that matter more.

But this concept of work leaves so much out.

In actuality, work itself can—and should—be a source of joy. It can offer the opportunity for purpose and meaning, for challenge and learning, and for great friendships. We deserve nothing less, and a shift in our expectations can make a big difference in terms of creating this sense of fulfillment.

## The Importance of a Joyful Work Experience

A great work experience is important, partly because it influences so many aspects of our lives. If we spend 80 percent of our time at work, simple math suggests that it will have an outsize influence on our lives. But as the line blurs between being on and off the clock, work continues to influence our personal lives. According to the American Psychological Association, it spills over, and in my own research in *Bring Work to Life by Bringing Life to Work*, I found work-life challenges affect both men and women, both mothers and fathers, and all generations. In addition, work-life challenges are not reserved for those who are married or those with children. The work-life conundrum is something that almost everyone goes through at some point in their lives.

Our experiences at work matter to our lives at work but also to our lives in general. It's impossible to share our best selves with our families, friends, and life partners if we're struggling with incivility or high levels of stress at work.

▶ One study in *Occupational Health Science* found work stress tends to negatively affect our sleep.

▶ Email also has an effect. A study published in the *Journal of Organizational Behavior* focused on incivility and found that when messages are rude or unnecessarily urgent, employees tend to experience adverse physical symptoms, negative emotions, and spillover of stress they bring home to their partners.

▶ Additional research reported by the American Psychological Association found that stress at work also affects parenting. Mothers who experience incivility at work tend to feel less effective overall, resulting in more strict, authoritarian parenting, which in turn correlates with adverse effects for their children.

▶ Another research effort at the Wharton School found that if parents are unavailable to children because of long hours or work distractions, children experience negative outcomes. And just having your device within sight can cause you to lose focus on the people around you, according to a study by the University of Texas. Truly being present with the people around you sends a message you care and they are your priority, and distraction can degrade the interaction and the relationship.

When work lacks joy, it can have far-reaching ripple effects. The opposite is also true. When work goes well, it can have impressive positive implications for the rest of our lives.

Troubled times can cause us to look at things differently, and new and expanded points of view are generally a good thing. In fact, the roots of the word "emergency" come from the Latin *emergere*, meaning to rise up or out. Especially now, in the new landscape of work, joy is critically important to our overall well-being. True happiness and joy are greater and richer than just contentment. They are based on internal perspectives rather than external conditions and tend to be more long-lasting. Joy and deep happiness are related to feelings of awe and peace, but they are also multifaceted. We can experience joy as a result of tough challenges or painful conditions that we have survived. Most of all, joy is something we are empowered to create. Far from something we simply hope to receive or for which we wait passively, joy is an experience we can embrace, foster, catalyze, and cultivate.

## What's New

This updated edition includes plenty of new ideas to help you create the conditions for happiness.

> ► What it (really) means to be happy at work
>
> ► How work can be a source of joy
>
> ► Whether work should be your identity (or not!)
>
> ► How to rethink self-care
>
> ► Stories about people who took action to create the conditions for happiness
>
> ► Key ideas you can put into practice for your own joyful work

This fresh new material—in addition to the previous substance of the book—will keep you moving forward to create happiness in your work and joy in your life.

**Let's start now!**

# Bonus Chapter

## CHOOSING WORK:
## THE SURPRISING CASE
## FOR WORK AS A SOURCE
## OF HAPPINESS

We're in the midst of a great rethink about work, with work at the forefront of our consideration as individuals and as societies. We've proven we can work from anywhere, and all over the world, we're reimagining how work gets done and what it means to us—including its priority in our lives.

Almost everyone must work to support themselves or their families, but people are increasingly selective about the organizations and leaders they choose to work for and the extent to which they invest their time, energy, and effort. People want and deserve great work, and their criteria for what constitutes great work, where they can have positive, fulfilling experiences, are consistently increasing, escalating, and expanding.

At the same time, there is an open assault on work. The popular press and social media glorify "quiet quitting" and "bare minimum Mondays." At their best, these are appropriate ways to manage boundaries and ensure we're not overextending or burning out. But more often, they undermine the benefits of work. We all have an instinct to matter, and work is an essential way we express skills and talents and contribute to our communities.

Specific work situations may not be ideal, but by vilifying or denigrating work generally, we miss the opportunity to empower ourselves, influence for the better, and embrace its positive impacts on life. We can create the conditions for happiness at work and advocate that leaders and organizations do the same. We can hold space for healthy boundaries and have fulfilling experiences on both sides.

Work will never go back to the way it was, and this is probably a good thing, but we can learn from where we've been and remind ourselves about the rewards of work going forward.

## What Is Happiness Anyway?

Happiness is one of the most sought-after experiences: We want joy in our personal lives, delight in our work, and bliss in our relationships. But happiness can also be elusive, and it's unrealistic to think you can achieve total happiness every day throughout all aspects of your life.

A better approach is to consider what happiness really means and reflect on how you experience it, then create the conditions for more of those situations to take hold.

## THE SPILLOVER EFFECT

Despite how elusive it can be, happiness is one of the most universally recognized emotions. Research published in the *Psychological Bulletin* found when people interact across cultures, happiness is one of the most familiar emotions and the one that tends to give people a sense of unity and camaraderie.

In addition, happiness is something people experience across life circumstances. It's not limited to a container of work or life. When you're happy with your work, you tend to experience greater levels of happiness in the rest of your life. The opposite is also true—when you're happier outside work, you tend to have a spillover effect and perceive greater happiness with your work. As a result, when you create the conditions for happiness at work, it will pay off for you in the rest of your life. And ironically, when you're intentional about the time you spend outside work and do things that bring you joy there, you'll also reap the benefits in your job. You can take action and be intentional, and it will matter across the boundaries of your life and work.

## HAPPY EXPERIENCES

But with all the focus on happiness at work, it's important to know that great work experiences are more complex and nuanced than having a sense of pure euphoria every day. You can have ups and downs, good days and bad days (or weeks!), and still have an overall sense of joy and satisfaction with your work.

No choice will result in nirvana. Whether it's the type of work you do, the hours you work, or the organization you work for, every choice is a set of circumstances. Some will be terrific, and others not so much. Every day, you make small decisions to engage or detach in terms of your work. As you do, it's wise to be intentional about your approach and reflective about what happiness at work actually is.

Here's what I would recommend you consider, alongside some tips on how to nurture joy.

### HAPPINESS IS DEDICATION

When we're happy at work, we experience dedication—that feeling of working hard and committing to our efforts. When you persevere in solving a problem or when you are conscientious about pointing out an issue and taking initiative to resolve it, you're dedicated. When you are loyal to a team or feel a level of allegiance to the organization, you're experiencing dedication.

In a study of five thousand people by the Muse, an online

career platform, quiet quitting was found to have a negative effect on happiness and brain health, with people suffering from worsening memory, focus, sleep, mood, productivity, and creativity. It seems detaching from your role, giving up, or failing to do your fair share results in deterioration of well-being. It's better to commit and dedicate yourself. And if you're not happy, it's best to take action and make another choice rather than simply surrendering.

Even if you're not in an idyllic role at the moment, do your best, and invest in bringing your best. By doing so, you'll feel more empowered and in control, but you'll also build your credibility and your relationships with others who know they can count on you.

## HAPPINESS IS IMMERSION

When you feel greater happiness at work, you also tend to feel immersed. You get going on a project and lose track of time. You're absorbed and feel embedded in the work. This is similar to the experience of flow in which your brain becomes focused on performing a task. During that time, there is less blood flow to the centers of your brain that concern themselves with judging others or yourself. In a state of flow or immersion, you're single-minded and homed in on accomplishing something.

A brilliant way to immerse yourself is to take initiative to learn something new or jump into a project that is outside your comfort zone or current areas of expertise. When you're working hard and learning, you're more likely to feel happy because you're expanding your capabilities and exploring new things. You're immersed in mastering something new.

Immerse yourself in your work, and feel good about the commitment you're making and the positive impacts you're having on others who rely on you.

## HAPPINESS IS VIBRANCY

Another characteristic of happiness at work is feeling energized—you literally feel more invigorated when you're happier. This energy tends to run in two directions: You're energized by what you're doing, and you want to invest energy in turn. You're inspired by something, and your determination makes you want to invest time and effort in solving a problem.

Vibrancy can come from the people around you as well. Research at the University of Chicago has found that when people around you are energized and engaged, you tend to be more motivated as well. And when people on your team are performing well, it tends to amp up the performance of the whole group.

Nurture your curiosity. Ask yourself questions, and investigate things you don't already know. Focus on being inquisitive broadly—across many topics—as well as deeply, in which you seek more substantive knowledge in a few key areas. Curiosity is one of the most in-demand skills today, so in addition to expanding your happiness, you'll also grow your career.

## HAPPINESS IS MATTERING

When you're happy, you are also likely to feel like your work matters and—even more—like you matter as well. A sense of purpose is driven by feeling there is a bigger picture outside yourself and that you are uniquely able to contribute to it. True purpose is also characterized by a feeling you're making a difference to real people, not just to corporate results. It's the work you do on the new customer interface that makes a client's experience a little easier or the marketing program you work on that entertains someone or brightens their day in addition to driving sales.

Clarify the meaning of your work and how it ladders up to the overall purpose of the organization. Recognize colleagues, knowing you're contributing to a culture of appreciation from which you'll benefit as well. Pay attention to what coworkers need from you, and follow through impeccably, knowing your work will affect their work, others' work, and so on.

## A HAPPY FUTURE

It's a misconception that pursuing happiness for its own sake is a good idea. There are two reasons for this. First, looking for happiness reminds you of what you don't have rather than what you have already that you can be grateful for today. Second, pursuing happiness for its own sake tends to focus on your own needs. Instead, when you focus on contributing to others' needs and making a difference to your community, you're more likely to feel a sense of joy.

Instead of chasing happiness as its own end, create the conditions for joyful work and life by committing to meaningful effort—immersing yourself, investing energy, and reminding yourself of how your work matters. All of these will help you accomplish greater happiness today and over time.

▶ REFLECT:

In what ways do others rely on you for the work you do?

_____

_____

_____

_____

_____

_____

_____

_____

_____

_____

## Work as a Source of Joy

So you know when you're happy, you tend to feel dedicated, immersed, energized, and fulfilled. But is work really a significant source of these, on par with vacations, time at the beach, or ice cream? The answer is a resounding yes.

And it goes beyond these experiences as well. There is deep value to be had from work based on the contribution you make, the impact you have, the connections you foster, and the meaning you can derive from it. No matter where you're working or how you're working—face-to-face, hybrid, remote, full-time, part-time, gig, or anything else—work is not only a fundamental part of a full life, it is also a pathway to happiness.

This is the significant value it provides.

## PURPOSE

Work provides a critical sense of meaning. Any company knows that to deliver powerful results, they must ensure people have a sense of shared purpose and aligned objectives, but purpose is also important for individuals. When people have it, they benefit from greater well-being, longevity, and self-esteem.

Work connects you with the bigger picture and gives you something to strive toward—something for which it's necessary to deliver your talents, skills, and unique abilities. Even if the work you're doing isn't a deep source of intrinsic passion, making the commitment, showing up, and following through for coworkers or customers is a source of meaning. Working with others reminds you of how your talents matter and of the positive ways in which others depend on your outcomes, your deliverables, and your follow-through. Being together in our work unites us in something bigger than ourselves.

Work also offers focus and importance. Without expectations each day, people can lose themselves in binge-watching, browsing, surfing, or doomscrolling. It can be tough to feel engaged when no one is counting on your work products or your follow-up. Productivity is higher when we know others are counting on us. And when we're productive, we tend to feel a greater sense of self-esteem, because we're achieving outcomes and doing something that matters. In addition, when you feel an obligation to a community—and know your contribution is needed for the group to succeed—it is good not only for motivation but for well-being.

Appreciate work for all the ways it links you with something outside yourself.

## CONNECTIONS

Work is fundamental to our sense of connection and community. We are social creatures, and we crave connections with other people. Depending on personality, people may prefer more or less closeness and time with others, but everyone needs some level of connectedness for physical, cognitive, and emotional well-being.

In addition, even superficial interactions are correlated with happiness, but the ease of ordering coffee with the app or receiving deliveries on our doorsteps is reducing our most rudimentary interactions with others. We have elevated convenience over connection, and people are feeling it. A poll by YouGov found people in every generation are struggling with a lack of friends and a decline in the number of close relationships in their life. But in the same study, 75 percent of people said work was one of the primary places they make friends, so it's a terrific venue not only for positive superficial interactions but also for creating and sustaining friendships. Within this context, work is becoming an increasingly important place to share, learn, and relate with others—all of which are linked with greater joy.

There are a few reasons for this. First, work provides continuity. Even though many people shift jobs and companies every year or two, work still offers an extended period through which to gain familiarity with others—getting to know them over time. Researcher Jeffrey Hall found it takes between sixty and two hundred hours of investment to make a good friend, and work can provide for this amount of interaction through the course of our shared tasks.

Work also provides a way for us to interact both on tasks (working on the project together or developing the report) as well as on relationships (running into each other at the coffee machine or chatting at the start of the virtual meeting). And work allows for an ebb and flow and the ups and downs in life. You see your colleague after they've just celebrated their child's graduation or on the tired mornings when they're struggling with training their new puppy.

Work is the perfect place to make friends and sustain them based on the time we spend and the relationships we form through tasks and personal interaction and over good times and bad, contributing to the richness of relationships.

We need each other based on interdependencies, but we also understand ourselves based on our relationships with others. We are coworkers, colleagues, and team members. Working together feeds this need for togetherness whether we're creating a new idea, solving a thorny problem, nodding to a friend across the cafeteria, or having an exchange with a teammate via instant messaging.

Working together also tends to energize us. Sociologists refer to this as emotional contagion or the bandwagon effect. It is the rush you get when you're with others, sharing together, and pulling in the same direction. It is the harmony you feel with laughter or applause. It's the power of a crowd to sweep us up and contribute to enthusiasm and momentum. Work can deliver this based on how we show up together with mutual goals in mind.

From the earliest times, people gathered in places for common purposes—whether it was for celebration, mourning, childcare, or learning. People have always gathered, and they have always come together to inspire a sense of community. In the modern world, work offers this esprit de corps. We walk in the door with another employee, show up on our video call with a coworker, or connect with someone while waiting for the elevator or the virtual meeting to start.

Embrace work for the connectedness it offers.

## STRETCH

Another key component of work is the challenge it offers, and when you're challenged, you're typically happier. In fact, the harder you work for something, the more joy and satisfaction you'll experience when you accomplish it.

As humans, we are fundamentally creative and want to contribute to what's new and impactful. In addition, companies live and die on the ability to adapt and respond to customers and the market in new ways. We can be creative in many parts of life, but our work is especially effective for stimulating thinking.

We are also energized by variety, and work provides it. Neuroscience research proves our brains are easily bored and crave a diversity of experiences. Work is a source of stimulation based on projects, challenges, and problems to solve. Of course, you can go rock climbing or shark diving in your personal life, but work is also a uniquely rich source of various opportunities through which we can express ourselves and stretch. It's the project you're struggling with and the learning you're doing by facing the latest customer challenge. Through these kinds of efforts, you're recognizing capabilities you may not have known you had, you're building skills, and you're likely bonding with others who are in the trenches with you.

The 15 percent rule suggests you'll be most motivated when you succeed only about 85 percent of the time. If you succeed more than this, you may conclude you have mastered a skill, and you'll want to move on to something new. If you succeed less than 85 percent of the time, you may decide the activity isn't the best fit for you, but if you succeed about 85 percent of the time and fail about 15 percent, it will keep you coming back for more. You'll want to strive to accomplish the goal and push to the next level of performance.

Seek opportunities to try new things, solve tough issues, and value work for the chance to grow.

▶ **REFLECT**

In what ways does your work provide you with opportunities to connect with others?

_____

_____

_____

_____

_____

_____

_____

_____

_____

_____

_____

_____

_____

_____

_____

_____

_____

_____

_____

## Should Work Be Your Identity Though?

Work is also an important part of your identity and your sense of self. You tend to understand yourself through many lenses—your race, ethnicity, religion, and regional culture—but also based on your roles, personality and characteristics, abilities, interests, beliefs, and the things that motivate you. Another primary way you form your sense of identity is based on your affiliations and sense of belonging.

When you have a strong sense of identity, you also tend to have higher levels of confidence and well-being. You tend to feel greater senses of pride, ownership, motivation, and control over your circumstances. In addition, a sense of identity tends to be linked with an ability to support others, arising from having a solid foundation of your own.

Work can be damaging if it's all-encompassing or toxic, but outside these negative conditions, work is an important part of a full life. While trying a new hobby, catching up with your best friend, or spending time immersed in a good book are all terrific ways to refresh, work is also a source of meaning and fulfillment. Even when work isn't ideal, it is an important way to express skills and talents, contribute to the broader community, and experience meaning and purpose.

Perhaps surprisingly—given the negative narratives about work—global research by Gallup found about 80 percent of people enjoy their work. A survey by LiveCareer found 87 percent of respondents believe their work is an important part of their life. In addition, 88 percent said their work is meaningful and they like their job. Fully 85 percent were satisfied with their work, and 88 percent felt it had value for its own sake.

So should work be a critical part of your identity? Is it healthy if it is? Consider the concepts of centrality, alignment, and dimensionality.

## CENTRALITY

It is valid that work can be central to your identity. You think of yourself as a lawyer, a designer, or a researcher. These can be healthy ways to understand yourself, and they are linked with purpose—how you understand the why of your contribution.

But beware a situation where work becomes absolute. When your career helps define you in addition to your other roles in life—as a volunteer, a parent, a partner, or a friend—great. But if work starts to overshadow everything else, it's time to reassess and likely pull back on the extent to which work is defining your life.

## ALIGNMENT

When your work is aligned with your values, you'll tend to feel a positive sense of identity associated with it. For example, you significantly value learning, intellect, and education, and your role on the faculty at a university is well aligned with this value. But if you're philosophically opposed to fossil fuels and advocate for a departure from traditional energy sources at the same time that you're working at an oil and gas company, you may struggle with being out of alignment.

Happiness is driven by greater alignment between what you love to do and what you have to do, and it is also significantly influenced by the extent to which your values are reinforced in the time you spend working.

## DIMENSIONALITY

Dimensionality is another aspect to consider in your identity. When you have more sources of meaning in your life and when they are diverse but related to each other, you'll tend to experience the greatest happiness.

For example, you may work at an art gallery, and you enjoy doing pottery with your best friend in your spare time. You also love hiking with your family on the weekends, and nature is a primary source of inspiration in your creative pursuits in pottery as well as the choices you make toward more nature-inspired art at the gallery. The variety of activities you enjoy linked by your passions helps you feel more satisfied.

You can achieve dimensionality by reflecting on what you value and taking steps to spend time doing what you love, and when you can create the conditions for aspects of your life to reinforce each other, it is especially powerful.

The disruption of work in the last few years has created a significant opportunity to reconsider and reimagine the experience of work and its meaning. Reflect on how happiness feels, embrace the value of work, and consider how work contributes to who you are as an important part of a fulfilled experience.

► **REFLECT**

In what ways are your values reflected in what you love to do?

_____

_____

_____

_____

_____

_____

_____

_____

_____

_____

_____

_____

_____

# 1

# CHOOSING JOY

Work can be joyful, but it can also be weighed down with myths that we must dispel. Despite what you might think, it's about more than work-life balance; there is an alternative view. Our brains also have a bearing on our joyful experiences, and we can create joy through cultivating the right kinds of experiences with our work.

## Creating Joy

Joy at work isn't something we should wait for. True happiness is something we can choose and create. When you're selecting a company, leader, or job, you can choose joy. When you're influencing your responsibilities and working together with colleagues, you can choose happiness. And when you're making sense of your work, you can choose a joyful approach.

While this empowerment is heady, it can also be daunting. As the quote says, "Our deepest fear is not that we are inadequate. Our deepest fear is that we are powerful beyond measure." If we're capable of choosing joy, then we are also *responsible* for our joy.

In terms of responsibility, it's a both-and situation. As individuals, we can appreciate this concept of agency—that we are agents of our own future. But there is also structure, the social systems and organizational systems that dictate many of our experiences. It is fair that we consider both but also that we realize "they are us." We can influence other people, we can lead—even if we are not formal leaders—and we can demonstrate our values. Socially speaking, the most important way people learn is through modeling—through observing other people—so we have greater influence than we may even realize, simply through demonstrating our values and inspiring joy in our own work.

▶ REFLECT

In what ways do you influence others?

_____

_____

_____

# Avoiding the Myths

In the world of popular culture, there are a lot of voices claiming to have the best formula to achieve work-life fulfillment. However, much of this cacophony is just noise. In fact, a lot of our understanding of work-life fulfillment is nothing but myth. Some such myths include the following.

**The myth of drudgery.** We tend to think of work as must-do drudgery. But in fact, work is a valuable part of our lives. In *Being Mortal*, Atul Gawande makes the point that one of the worst things we can hear is that we're no longer needed or that our contribution is no longer a critical part of society. At its best, work should be fulfilling, and we should keep our expectations high for the role it plays in our lives. At a minimum, work is a means to important ends like providing for our families or paying for activities that allow us to grow and enjoy life. Either way, work doesn't have to equal a negative experience. It can be a rewarding pursuit.

**The myth of sacrifice.** Another problem with the work-life discussion is that it points to sacrifice. According to popular lore, we can't have everything, but in truth, we *can* have it all—just not all at once. There are seasons of life, and some will be busier than others. While you're building your career and juggling your job, family, and self, things will be more challenging than when you're winding down and struggling to ensure that your contribution is still relevant. Enjoy where you are, and know that you *will* have it all over time—even if you won't have it all at once.

**The myth of separation.** Fundamentally, work is part of a full life. While we may think we want to relax on an island for the rest of our lives, this may not be true for the longer term. (After all, how much relaxing can one person really do?) In a fascinating series of studies published in the *Journal of Applied Psychology*, people were asked whether they would still work if they won the lottery. The proportion of people saying yes varied over the years between 80 percent and about 66 percent. Some years it was higher, and some years it was lower, but overall, people regularly report that they want to continue working even if they don't have to for financial reasons. Work is important because it's part of our lives and a critical way we contribute to society and feel valuable.

**The myth of perfection.** One of the most damaging myths is the idea that there is a perfect job or career and that whatever we have today isn't enough. While striving for the next great thing is a unique part of being human, being satisfied with what we have is critical to happiness as well. In reality, your current role is an opportunity for learning and growth, whether the challenge is to excel in a perfect-fit job or to survive where you are until you can make a move.

**The myth of value.** Another myth our popular culture fosters is the idea that some work is inherently more valuable than other work. This is bunk. All work has dignity and value, no matter what kind of work it is. Recently, I engaged with a client who believed the most important work of their organization happened in the field, where they supported those in need. Unfortunately, this client was inadvertently devaluing the efforts of everyone else in the office who was supporting the field agents. *All work matters*, even if it is upstream from the jobs most closely connected to the end user or customer.

Getting entangled in the myths of work and life can be disorienting and disheartening, but the realities are much more simple and meaningful. Work should be fulfilling, and you can have it all. Work and life are both parts of a whole experience, and there is enough great work to go around. In addition, there is no perfect role, but all work—no matter what kind—has importance and dignity.

▶ REFLECT

Which of the work-life myths have affected your thinking?

---

---

---

---

# Better Than Balance

The discussions about work-life balance have reached a fever pitch recently, and it is certainly a critical concern to ensure work has meaning and that it's not undermining your life, your spirit, or your sense of value. It's vital that we continue to find solutions to the work-life challenge, but the concept of balance has never been enough. It's too limiting.

So what's wrong with balance? And what are the alternatives?

**First, work-life balance artificially separates work and life.** Work is part of a fulfilling life, and work and life should be integrated as part of a whole experience. Even if your job doesn't give you shivers of joy with each new day, working is part of what each of us does and the contribution we make to society. In an ideal circumstance, work would provide purpose and meaning, but at a minimum, it is a reason to wake up in the morning, and it is a paycheck that helps support us and our families.

**Second, work-life balance suggests a precariousness that isn't helpful.** A goal to balance suggests that things are *hanging in the balance* or could easily get *off balance*, causing bad outcomes. It is more constructive to think of solutions that continue to evolve over shifts in life and work. Rather than falling or failing, you may have good days or better days or not-so-good days. These variations are normal, and it's more useful to think of life as always evolving and changing from day to day or year to year rather than as a high-risk enterprise where things could go wrong with one misstep.

**Third, work-life balance doesn't think big enough.** We deserve more than just balance. We deserve work-life fulfillment, harmony, and satisfaction. If we set the bar too low, we won't demand enough of ourselves, our leaders, and our companies. The opportunity is to believe that you can have more. Rather than having to make forced choices between two priorities, *believe that everything is possible.*

How we talk to ourselves matters, and how we talk about issues makes a difference. Let's bury "work-life balance" and think bigger and better about work-life fulfillment in order to do a little less balancing and a lot more joyful living.

▶ REFLECT

How has the concept of balance shaped your opinions about your work and life?

_____

_____

_____

_____

_____

_____

## Joy and Brain Science

We know more today about how the brain works than ever before, and in addition to being extraordinarily interesting, our knowledge of this realm can help us have better experiences.

You can use brain science to inform how you think, how you work, and where you work. Being intentional about all these can help you love what you do and be even more effective and cultivate joy.

**Go deep.** In his book *The Shallows*, Nicholas Carr demonstrates how our internet usage has rewired our brains. We think superficially, skimming, glancing, and scanning rather than reading or processing more deeply. Cal Newport, in his book *Deep Work*, advocates for focusing, contemplating, and concentrating. His contention is that this distraction-free thinking has become increasingly rare and is a skill we must learn (or relearn). In fact, empathy—so critical to our humanity—is impossible without deeply considering others' situations, and the ability to solve problems and develop ideas cannot happen effectively without a depth of thought.

**Take breaks.** Many people avoid taking breaks in the name of efficiency—working through lunch and avoiding the break room except to recaffeinate for the next meeting. In fact, breaks are important to help the brain recharge, particularly breaks away from the office, according to a study in the *Scandinavian Journal of Work and Organizational Psychology*. Another study in the *Academy of Management Journal* shows it's also impactful when you have your own choice of what to do during your lunch breaks. Rather than taking the obligatory "working lunch," being able to choose your activity is helpful to recovering your energy.

**Get moving.** Our brains are also wired for the movement of our bodies. Research at Oregon Health and Science University found quick bursts of exercise can boost memory and learning. Take a walk, stretch, or get away from your desk for a round of jumping jacks. (If suddenly rising from your desk for rowdy activity might be career-limiting in your company, by all means, find a private space for this one.)

**Socialize.** Our brains are most rejuvenated and ready for the next task when we take time for socializing. One study published in the *International Journal of Nursing Studies* demonstrated nurses who took breaks to socialize with colleagues had reduced stress and were less likely to leave their jobs. Another study published in the *Journal of Organizational Behavior* showed taking breaks with a social focus tended to reduce negative emotions during the workday.

**Find green spaces.** A large amount of research summarized in *Science Advances* has suggested the importance of nature for our brains to function optimally. One of the most recent studies, at the University of Washington, pointed to enhanced cognitive function and mental health when people were exposed to nature.

In fact, another study published in the *Journal of Environmental Psychology* found microbreaks—quick moments away from a task—looking at a roof planted with greenery helped improve performance in a task requiring attention and accuracy.

**Go toward the light (but not too much blue light).** One of the most requested features in offices is access to natural light. In addition to the natural human desire for light and views, natural light has been proven by studies published in the *JBI Library of Systematic Reviews* to have positive effects on health, stress, and productivity. Compared to full-spectrum natural light, ongoing research published in *Applied Ergonomics* shows that blue light—the light at the beginning of the light spectrum and that comes over the horizon first at daybreak—tends to suppress melatonin and tell the brain to "turn on." This has implications for sleep and circadian rhythms. Too much blue light—the kind that is emitted from devices—has many negative impacts, leading to everything from depression and disrupted sleep to obesity. For better sleep and health, reduce exposure to blue light, especially at night.

► REFLECT

Which of these experiences have you had before?

_____

_____

# Unexpected Sources of Happiness

In addition to the sources of happiness based on brain science, there are also some proven sources of positivity that may surprise you.

**Do some art (even if you're not an artist).** A study published in *PLOS One* found that visual art production changes your brain and as a result can enhance your resilience and happiness, reducing pressure and increasing your well-being physically, emotionally, and cognitively. Additional research at Drexel University found that when people engaged in creative activities—even coloring or doodling—the pleasure centers of their brains were further activated. They were literally increasing blood flow in their brains' reward regions, contributing to greater feelings of happiness and self-confidence. The effects were true for both artists and nonartists. So doodle in a meeting, or try your hand at watercolor in your free time. You'll enhance your sense of joy regardless of your talent level.

**Spend time wisely.** If you want to be happy, you'll also do well to spend your time on activities that are both relaxing and rejuvenating. Research at the University of Nottingham found that spending time on a hobby you enjoy or whiling away the hours playing games is correlated with happiness. Taking naps is also a great way to boost your happiness.

And interestingly, research at the University of Colorado

found that setting your alarm to wake up an hour earlier each day (assuming you're getting enough sleep overall) is also correlated with happiness—likely because you have more control over your time and because you can fill your day with more of what you love to do.

**Invest in experiences.** In creating the conditions for happiness, it's also smart to seek experiences that are meaningful. While you can spend money on items or objects, experiences are much more likely to pay off in your sense of joy or contentment. This is because purchasing things tends to offer only fleeting satisfaction, while experiences tend to engage you over time and in multiple parts of your sensory brain circuits. You enjoyed sightseeing in Venice, tasting great meals, and feeling the rocking of a gondola ride and the cobblestones under your feet while you walked throughout the city. These experiences make memories, which are more lasting than objects can deliver. In addition, experiences are usually enjoyed with others, also making them greater sources of happiness. The memory of the skydiving you did with your son will live on for you, delivering a dose of joy each time you recall those moments.

**Eat your veggies.** If you're a picky eater, you can move on to the next source of happiness, but for all the healthy eaters (or wannabe healthy eaters), this will likewise make you happy: Studies at the University of Warwick found greater consumption of fruits and vegetables was correlated with greater happiness. A related study at the University of Leeds hypothesized that the greater presence of carotenoids in the blood is what contributed to greater senses of subjective well-being when people ate more healthfully.

**Contribute to your community.** Another sure pathway to happiness is strong connections with your community. This can be with children, as a study published in *Social Psychological and Personality Science* demonstrated. Those who put children's needs ahead of their own experienced greater happiness. Of course, you must still set healthy boundaries for children, but selfless investments in children's well-being through spending time and demonstrating unconditional love were strongly linked with greater happiness.

You can also volunteer in your community to experience greater happiness. People all have an instinct to matter and crave the opportunity to contribute their talents and skills to their communities. This was born out by a study at the University of Illinois, which found when people saw others whose needs were fulfilled, they felt happier themselves. In short, boosting others boosts you as well.

**Look beyond money.** It's a misconception that money can buy happiness. Everyone needs a threshold level of income to ensure safety, adequate food, and shelter, but these result in only baseline satisfaction. Beyond this threshold, money won't buy additional happiness. True joy tends to result from all the other factors discussed above—from purpose and health to making meaningful contributions to the community.

**Get a pet.** Another great idea for enhancing your happiness is to get a pet. A study of over six thousand participants by researchers at the University of York and the University of Lincoln found pets help reduce stress. This is partially because they provide emotional support and because they are tuned in to humans. Brain scans of dogs at Emory University demonstrated that dogs are especially sensitive to human cues, helping to explain why their companionship is so meaningful—they are tuned in to us in ways other humans may not be. Research by the Kennel Club Charitable Trust found 87 percent of people said having a dog makes them a better, happier version of themselves.

In the end, you don't need to simply wait for happiness to blossom around you. Instead, you can create the conditions for your own happiness, and taking positive action can be its own source of happiness as well.

► **REFLECT**

Which of these sources of happiness is most surprising to you?

_____

_____

## HAPPINESS IN PRACTICE

▸ Mariah was feeling a little down and decided to apply some brain science for her well-being. She started biking to her train stop each day, benefiting from the immersion in nature and the movement at the beginning and ending of her days. While she was at the office, she made plans to walk with a friend during breaks at work. On nice days, they walked outside, and on days when the weather was less than lovely, they walked around the office. While they caught some strange looks at first, they also started a bit of a trend at their office—toward breaks and time with colleagues to get away from their desks and get moving.

## HAPPINESS IN ACTION

▸ Manage your mindset, avoiding the myths of happiness and reflecting on your own thinking.

▸ Be intentional about the choices you make—both large and small—about how you spend your time.

▸ Know that you can create the conditions for happiness based on your own decisions.

# 2

# CHOOSING PURPOSE

Create joy by focusing on your purpose and pursuing your passions, but also consider your perspectives. In addition, choose to embrace happiness by fostering plenty of optimism.

## The Power of Purpose

We've all heard about how important purpose is to both organizations and people, but as work changes and hybrid work models become the norm, purpose has renewed importance. Beyond the what, where, when, and how of work, it can focus us on the why, and this is motivational.

In addition, purpose contributes powerfully to happiness. In fact, research published in the *Journal of Happiness Studies* found that when participants felt a greater sense of purpose, they tended to feel more positive emotions—specifically content-ment, relaxation, enthusiasm, and joy. And they felt less angry, anxious, sluggish, or sad. They also reported greater satisfaction with life and overall well-being.

Many other studies have also linked purpose with all kinds of benefits from reduced mortality and incidence of cardiovas-cular disease to less loneliness.

Greater purpose was also correlated with better outcomes for companies—like growth, market expansion, and successful prod-uct launches. Employees reaped the benefits of more purpose-driven work experiences in terms of feeling like work was more meaningful, feeling happier, and being more productive.

## DEFINING PURPOSE

But what is purpose really? Generally, it is a belief that your life matters and that you make a difference. It is a sense of being guided by meaningful values and goals. Purpose can be related to families or parenting, career, religion, activism, artistic pur-suits, or other contributions to community. In Japanese, the word *ikigai* describes a reason for being or a reason to wake up in the morning.

Purpose doesn't have to be world-changing either. It can simply be the expression of your talents to help your family or your friends. One woman expressed her *ikigai* as the need and desire to make soup for her family.

Purpose doesn't have to include pressure to find the cures for diseases or inspire world peace. It can just be doing the next thing that makes sense and performing work that allows you to express your unique capabilities to help others or contribute to the broader community.

## THE IMPORTANCE OF ALIGNMENT

A key element of purpose is alignment. We will be most engaged in our work when the mission and goals of the organization also matter to us and when we feel like we can make a contribution to the bigger picture. We all want to build castles, not just lay bricks.

For example, working on an industrial line making hardware (think hooks and doorknobs) makes a contribution to our collective need for beauty and efficiency in our environments. Serving coffee at a diner contributes to people's opportunities to come together in conversation and community. The accounting clerk who processes payments at the university is contributing to students' learning and paving the way for them to reach their goals.

While a strong purpose can work to motivate and engage, it can also help people choose and clarify their investments of time and effort. Years ago, I worked with Helen, who was morally opposed to an industry our company was serving. She asked to opt out of working on those accounts. We accommodated her, and she was able to contribute brilliantly to other accounts while team members who didn't share her concerns served the other account.

Or consider Josie, who quit her job at a well-known company because she didn't agree with what she perceived to be the negative impact they were having on the community. Purpose can help people and companies make choices that ensure the greatest match between values, talents, and contributions.

## WHY PURPOSE MATTERS SO MUCH

But there are additional reasons that purpose is connected to happiness, and these suggest how to be happier every day with a greater sense of meaning.

**Purpose focuses you.** Purpose provides an important sense of focus in what can be a chaotic world. There is a daily deluge of information from so many sources all at once, and attention has become one of the scarcest resources. But a sense of purpose can provide focus, giving you a reason for your actions.

Perhaps you show up for your job every day so you can provide for your children or create a stable life for you and your partner. Or maybe you're a purchasing agent, and the parts you source go into the production of walkers for the elderly, giving them mobility and quality of life. Perhaps you're a tax expert, and you prepare returns for clients who would otherwise be overwhelmed by the process on their own. All of these are meaningful ways you contribute your skills to others.

Despite all the noise, you can use purpose to focus, reminding yourself about why you wake up every morning—to provide for your family, to make a difference to your teammates, or to support your clients.

**Purpose grounds you.** A sense of awe has been linked with happiness. Awe is the feeling that you are in the presence of something greater than yourself. You're at the beach, and the crashing waves impress you, or you look at a sunset and feel inspired. Maybe you're on a mountain peak, and you're moved by the view, or the sound of a child's laughter gives you hope.

All these affect you by reducing blood flow to the part of your brain that is vigilant about yourself and how you're being perceived. You tend to feel small in the face of things that are grand, and this can give you a sense of liberation and happiness.

Purpose can do this as well. You feel like the work you do matters to someone, your small part of something has meaning, and you're empowered to act. You work on the cafeteria line at a university and check in with the students each day, helping them to feel seen and providing a touchstone for their well-being. You work through an issue with a customer who is upset and help them reduce their stress. You notice your teammate is struggling with a project and offer to guide them through the new system so they can get their work done and go home to their family on time.

To find happiness with purpose, consider what matters in the bigger picture and how your role can make a difference to others.

**Purpose connects you.** Feeling socially disconnected is one of the fastest routes to depression, anxiety, and other mental health challenges. It is also a sure path to physical health challenges. But happiness is linked with feeling part of a community, and so is purpose.

People feel the greatest sense of purpose when their work matters to others. The corporate goal to grow at 15 percent per year and the organizational objective to penetrate new markets are standard, but what truly motivates and engages people is clarity about how corporate growth or market penetration will help the community. Perhaps the new product will help mothers with quality of life for their children or bring friends together in new ways. Maybe the service your organization offers will make life easier for a struggling population somehow. Purpose is connected to people and the ways you're making a difference for others through the value chain of your work.

Give thought to how your work serves others, how it contributes to your team or to your client. Make your purpose personal, and it will be most effective in contributing to happiness as well.

## MEANINGFUL ACTION

In applying purpose, there are four key actions that matter most:

**Clarify your purpose.** Define your purpose with as much detail and clarity as possible, identifying what differentiates your purpose and what makes your contribution to it unique.

**Articulate your purpose.** Write down your purpose, and revisit it regularly to keep it fresh.

**Choose well.** Actively use purpose for choice making. No choice is ideal, but as individuals, we can choose a job or a volunteer effort or a task that is as close as possible to what matters most to us. And we can remind ourselves of how even small, everyday tasks build up to something bigger than ourselves.

**Stay nimble.** Monitor, measure, reevaluate, and reassess regularly. Circumstances and context will change, and you'll need to shift and adapt. This is resilience, and it will be important for the future of work generally and the work each of us does.

Purpose is a big deal, but it doesn't have to be rocket science. Keep the bigger picture in mind, and ensure actions are in alignment with what matters most to you. As the saying goes, "We are the choices we make." And "We are what we repeatedly do." Purpose should drive all these choices and actions, and we will be happiest and most fulfilled when our choices and actions are aligned with a clear purpose.

► **REFLECT**

In what ways does your work give you a sense of purpose?

# Following Your Passion

Purpose and passion are closely related. While purpose is your why, passion is what motivates and energizes you, and it is also closely linked with happiness.

Plenty of career coaches advise you to follow your passion, but it turns out this recommendation really is legitimate, and it's even supported by research.

Despite its validity, there is some pushback on passion. Some have questioned whether passion is enough to drive career success, and others have questioned whether passion is just a pipe dream. Perhaps it's better to just be pragmatic about your chances of employment and wage security.

But passion turns out to be a great accelerant for your career. Evidence published in the *Journal of Applied Psychology* from an eleven-year longitudinal study suggests when you tap into your passion, you're more likely to take actions that drive your growth and success.

# Discovering Your Passion

The process for figuring out what you're most passionate about can be mystifying, but it doesn't have to be. There are some straightforward ways to explore and discover what energizes you most.

**Embrace the first person.** First, when you consider what you love to do, put yourself in the first person. Imagine yourself in a situation you might love. Rather than considering the situation in the third person—from a distance or in the abstract—imagine yourself actually doing the tasks or activities associated with what you're considering.

An Ohio State University study found first-person envisioning fools the part of your brain that pays more attention to common biases or social judgments. Don't let limiting beliefs like "men are less suited for careers in early childhood education" or "women should steer away from the sciences" override your preferences. It turns out imagining yourself in situations can help you establish a more clear sense of your passions. This can—and should—shape your pursuits.

**Give yourself some advice.** Another helpful lens on your preferred path comes from the value of hindsight, which researchers at Clemson University studied. Ask yourself to consider a younger you, and give yourself advice. The value of perspective isn't new. George Land and Beth Jarman wrote about the power of thinking "backward from perfect" in their classic 1990s book *Breakpoint and Beyond*. Backward induction is a mathematical reasoning concept in which you place yourself in the future and then reason backward from that future point to facilitate decisions to get you there.

So in order to give yourself career advice, take a twist on backward induction, and start from what you know today and work backward. According to the Clemson study, the most compelling advice fell into the categories of education, self-worth, and relationships. So focus on these for a new perspective on your passion, and ask yourself the following:

- **My education.** What would I do differently in terms of my education? What has worked, and what can I build on? What am I curious about? In what areas might I continue to seek learning or development?
- **My self-worth.** What are my best contributions? In what situations have I felt most fulfilled and rewarded for my talents? What mistakes have I made, and what would it be wise to avoid in the future?
- **My relationships.** What people have been most helpful to me, and how might I build those or similar relationships? Which people have sucked me dry and should be avoided moving forward?

A wise colleague had a regular ritual where she and her husband, on their anniversary, would open a bottle of wine and reflect on their past year and set goals for the year to come. Another colleague would regularly create a vision board with his partner and then keep it in front of himself each day of the coming year. These are smart approaches to emulate—helping to keep purpose front and center in your life.

► REFLECT

What might you include on your own vision board?

_____

_____

_____

_____

_____

_____

_____

_____

_____

_____

_____

_____

_____

_____

_____

_____

_____

## HOW TO KNOW IF YOU'VE FOUND YOUR PASSION

You can determine whether you've hit upon your passion by tuning in to your thoughts and your feelings.

**Your thoughts.** In particular, when you are interested and curious about something and when you want to explore, learn more, and take action, these are signals you've identified a passion. In addition, when you're passionate about something, you may notice you're naturally good at it or you find yourself investing time in it, which makes you better as well.

For example, you discover information about agile work methods, and you take the ideas to your team, where you become the resident expert and ultimately a leader in agile practices for your organization.

**Your feelings.** You also know you've tapped into an area of passion when you feel energized by it. You get a sense of heightened emotion and vigor when you're learning and contributing in your chosen area. And when you're passionate, you're likely to feel connected to the bigger picture of your purpose—believing your efforts matter and link with your community.

For example, you're a tax accountant, and you're excited about the new ways you've found to apply a tax code and impact your clients or your company. Or you're in HR and especially enthusiastic about the development program you're rolling out to leaders and the ways it will positively affect their growth.

# TAPPING INTO PASSION

Passion is fuel for career success because it drives key actions and behaviors. Here are a few ways you can leverage your passion.

**Express professional courage.** People with passion tend to take risks in their chosen areas of interest. This can mean seeking knowledge in an area that is new to you—taking a class or looking for mentors in an effort to expand your awareness.

It can also mean expressing professional courage by trying a new method in your job, advocating for a new idea in a meeting, volunteering for a project outside your department, or applying for another role or promotion. All these are constructive ways to take risks and use the power of your passion.

**Persist.** According to the research, passion also helps you persist in the face of challenges. Career growth rarely happens on a straight, smooth course. It is much more likely to occur with fits and starts. You'll take a job working for a great leader, and then company reorganization may have you reporting to someone else. Or you'll get a couple promotions, followed by a plateau.

With passion guiding you, it's possible to persevere and stick with your interests despite ups and downs. You love your role in sales, and despite setbacks, you stay the course and ultimately get the annual award for strongest sales in a down market, capturing the attention of senior leadership and paving the way for your next opportunity.

**Align activities.** Interestingly, when you engage in activities outside work that bring you joy, you'll be more likely to perceive greater fulfillment within your work as well. So use your passion to motivate your volunteer or personal activities.

If you love engineering activities, volunteer to help with the pinewood derby in your community, or if you have strong environmental interests, get involved with your local community garden or watershed project.

**Consider your people.** Another reason passion is so significant is that it connects you with your people, and you are likely to feel happier when you also feel linked with your community. Statistically, people's career and volunteer choices tend to be representative of their personalities, so when you take on activities within your area, you'll be connecting with others who have similar interests, concerns, and priorities, which in turn will energize you even more.

## PAY ATTENTION

Finding your passion doesn't have to be hard. Just pay attention to what interests and energizes you. In addition, you don't necessarily have to have a grand plan or a road map for your entire life. Just make the day-to-day and month-to-month choices that align with what you enjoy and what you do well.

Spend time on what you like, what you do well, and activities that contribute to your community. These will add up to a life that brings you fulfillment and adds to others' fulfillment as well.

► REFLECT

What are the things that interest and energize you most?

_____

_____

_____

_____

_____

_____

_____

_____

_____

_____

_____

_____

_____

_____

_____

_____

_____

_____

# Perspective

You've given thought to your passion and reflected on your priorities, but what about your own perspectives? How you achieve purpose and your journey to fulfillment are as much mental as they are about your approach to your work. As the saying goes, "Change your thinking, change your life." Here's how.

**Empower yourself.** The most important thing to remember is you're empowered to create your own joy and purpose. I've said it before and will repeat it again because it's so important. *Don't fall into the trap of believing you must find just the right role to be fulfilled or that it's the responsibility of your boss or your company to create meaning for you.* Your work matters, and you can foster your purpose and create meaning *for yourself.*

**Focus on three things.** When people have a sense of purpose, they say it is the result of three elements. Having purpose is about feeling connected to something larger than yourself, knowing your work matters to that bigger thing, and realizing your work's importance to people. You want to contribute to your organization's financial results, sure, but it's really knowing how you affect people that will get you out of bed in the morning.

So how do you move toward these three elements of purpose? Make a mental logic train from your work to the things that matter most. Perhaps you handle applications in the college recruiting process. Your work matters to the students who are shaping their futures. If you welcome guests at the neighbor-hood fitness facility, you're making a difference in their positive feelings toward their health goals. You get the idea. Connect what you do, no matter what it is, to its broader significance and its impact on those around you.

**Be clear about your unique talent.** As you think about your contribution to the whole, remember how your talent is unique. Remind yourself how your unusual sense of humor lightens the day for everyone or how your second-to-none level of organization provides structure for things to get done effectively. Reinforcing how you bring special value to the whole is a big part of feeling fulfilled and purposeful at work.

**Think beyond your work.** As you're shaping your perceptions, remember your overall purpose in life is made up of more than just your work. You also serve your purpose through family, relationships with friends, and contributions to the community. Ironically, feeling a sense of purpose at work can also be built through considering your larger purpose *beyond* work. Factor in the nonwork contributions you make, like coaching Little League or building houses for low-income families on the weekends. When your purpose is met in multiple places—family, friends, community—it's that much easier for your work to feel satisfying because it's one part of a holistic perspective.

Ultimately, a change in perception requires self-awareness.

Surely the saying is true that when you change your thinking you change your life, and your purpose at work is a great place to start.

▶ **REFLECT**

In what ways do you bring unique value to those around you?

_____

_____

_____

_____

_____

_____

_____

_____

_____

_____

_____

_____

_____

_____

_____

_____

# Joy through Optimism

Optimism seems like a straightforward characteristic—a simple spotlight on what's good and future-focused—but it is actually quite a powerful attribute. From a longer life to better performance at work and satisfaction with your job, it has some seriously positive effects.

Optimism is helpful because those who are optimistic tend to bounce back more easily from difficult situations—they are more resilient. In addition, they are thought to have better control over their emotions and may make better overall choices about diet, exercise, and other habits such as tobacco use. When you face stress at work, an optimistic view can help you cope in healthy ways, or when you're passed over for the promotion, you'll be able to recover more easily and keep doing great work toward the next opportunity.

Optimism is related to a growth mindset, which means optimists believe they can change their circumstances. They are more likely to take positive actions to create their own futures rather than viewing themselves as having fixed sets of skills and traits that can't change or adapt. If you're facing an especially tough project at work, an optimistic approach can keep you motivated to try new solutions.

So you're sold on optimism, but how to be more optimistic? Here are a few tips.

**Be present.** One of the hallmarks of pessimism is worry about the future and negativism that can spiral out of control. One of the strategies for optimism is to stay more focused on the present. In fact, a study from MIT found middle school students who practiced mindfulness experienced less stress. Be present in each meeting and each interaction with colleagues. Focus and give your best in every moment, knowing that investment in the now will result in a positive future.

**Be grateful.** Another surefire way to increase your optimism is to be grateful for what you have. Gratitude has long been shown to improve physical and psychological health, increase empathy, reduce aggression, reduce stress, improve self-esteem, improve relationships, and even improve sleep. It is logical that gratitude is also associated with optimism. When you appreciate what you have, you have more positivity about all that is to come. Even when you're facing a problem that seems insurmountable, you can express gratitude and optimism. Whenever she faces a challenge, one of my colleagues says, "If this is my worst problem, I'm the luckiest woman in the world."

**Think long-term.** Another way to be more optimistic is to extend your time horizon. When you're facing a challenge that feels difficult in the moment, extend your view, and consider whether it will matter in a month or a year. The disagreement with a client or the conflict with a coworker may seem significant today but won't be a big deal after some time has passed. Being optimistic can be easier when you think of a bright future in which present problems won't even be on your radar screen.

**Manage your expectations.** One of the reasons for dissatisfaction is experience and expectation that don't match. Keep your expectations realistic in order to be more satisfied with what's going on around you. If you have set the bar too high—on your timing for the next raise or the juicy project you're sure will come your way—you may be disappointed. Set goals that keep you motivated, but be realistic to ensure you're delighted when opportunities emerge. This will keep you optimistic about the next opportunity and the next.

► REFLECT

What is something you're grateful for?

_____

_____

_____

_____

_____

_____

_____

_____

_____

## HAPPINESS IN PRACTICE

► Olivia and Emma were long-time colleagues, but their company had been through downsizing, and they were finding it tricky to stay positive. They noticed their conversations would frequently devolve into complaining. While this was helpful because they were sharing experiences and empathy, they realized they were also leaving their discussions feeling demotivated. They decided to take time at least once a week in their discussions to focus on something they were optimistic about. They took a few minutes regularly to share something they felt positively about for themselves, for each other, for others, or for their company. They said they felt more energized and more connected based on this shift in their time together.

## HAPPINESS IN ACTION

► Focus on your why and the big picture.
► Consider what energizes you most, as well as how you make a unique contribution to the people around you.
► Empower yourself to choose a positive outlook, even when you're facing challenge or difficulty.

# 3

# CHOOSING CULTURE

Creating joy and happiness is influenced by working in *your* right company and best-fit job—the one that offers the optimal mix of things you love and the responsibilities for which you're accountable, within a healthy culture.

## Choosing the Right Company

In an age when every company tells you it values work-life fulfillment, how can you tell whether a company means it? What will it really be like if you join the organization? If you're already part of a company, how can you help them practice what they preach? Here are a few ways to tell that a company truly values work-life fulfillment, along with some suggestions on how to bring any existing culture up to speed!

**Consider their policies and practices.** Ask about the company's specific policies and practices supporting work-life fulfillment. What are their approaches to vacation, leave, benefits, or work from home? Listen for what they have established formally (for example, as written policies) and informally (for example, as result of a particular leader's bent). If your leader changes (which is typical in corporate life), what policies will you have to fall back on? Be sure the written policies are robust enough to support work-life fulfillment even if your leadership shifts.

**Consider technology.** Determine what the company supplies in terms of tools and technology, and be sure they keep it up-to-date effectively. Find out what kinds of sharing platforms the company uses and whether you'll be able to use your preferred operating systems or whether they're standardized on something else. Consider not just hardware but also software and social media. Will you have a desktop publishing program or have to muddle through with basic packages? Will you be able to access social media now and then while you're at work, or does the company have firewalls that make that impossible? These kinds of questions are relevant to work-life fulfillment because software affects your efficiency and effectiveness (read: when you get your work done, you have more time for you), and social media can affect your connections with others outside work and therefore your quality of life.

**Watch how they work.** Learn more about how others at the company work. Their behavior is the best barometer of company norms, "what goes," and whether people can work alternative hours. Can people come in early on summer days and leave early once in a while to get to the beach or the golf course? Do people head out of the office to catch their daughter's soccer game and then turn on later in the evening to finish their project? Are people open and transparent about their working habits, or do they have to keep quiet about their lives outside work? Look for companies where people work hard to accomplish results but where they can do so with flexibility.

► REFLECT

What are some of the cues that signal culture within your organization?

_____

_____

_____

_____

_____

_____

## Assessing Your Job for the Right Proportions

It is extraordinarily rare to find a job you love 100 percent of the time. Unless you are in a minuscule minority of people, there will always be things you don't love about your work. You may love the travel your job requires but not tracking your expenses. The work you do with customers may challenge you, but the wining and dining may drain you. You may enjoy designing new solutions for your clients, but the processes of billing and invoicing irritate you.

The trick to loving what you do is all about proportions. How do you find work that includes more of what you love to do and less of what you don't?

Consider two elements of your work. First, there are things you love to do. Then, there are things you have to do. You can visualize these on a two-by-two diagram.

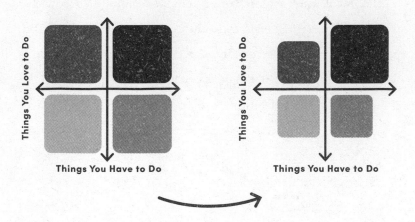

Finding work that is the best fit for you involves having as much overlap as possible between what you love to do and what you have to do, and the corollary—finding work that includes as little as possible of the things you don't enjoy.

Because every job will include both tasks you love and tasks you don't, here are key considerations as you seek your best-fit job.

**What is core to the job?** Consider what is core to the job versus what is peripheral. For example, working with numbers might be core to a financial role. Another role may be fundamentally about research, but annual budgeting is also part of your responsibilities. If what you don't love is core, you might need to consider a change. But if what you don't love is just an additional part of the duties, it may be something you'll need to learn to live with.

**What requires your time?** It is also helpful to consider how much time you have to spend on your tasks. A good rule of thumb is the 50 percent threshold. If what you love to do is what you're spending the majority of your time on, great. On the other hand, if the obligations you don't love are taking up most of your time, it might be a good idea to rethink your job choice.

**What's on your path?** Sometimes, you're in a job with a larger proportion of work you don't love, but you're on your way to bigger things. In this case, continue paying your dues and learn as much as you can in the trenches, even though your current proportion of work may not be compelling or stimulating. Keep your eye on the bigger prize, and buckle down.

**What does it take from you?** If the parts of your job that are necessary but not fulfilling sap your energy or run counter to your values, you may want to consider making an adjustment. Years ago, a superstar on my team asked never to work with a certain type of company because its values were antithetical to hers. We regularly assigned those consulting roles to others who didn't have the same disagreements. The bottom line: ensure the parts of your job that are necessary but not your favorite don't require you to compromise fundamental personal principles.

► REFLECT

How much overlap do you experience between what you have to do and what you love to do?

_____

_____

_____

_____

_____

_____

_____

_____

# The Wrong Mix

If you find that your mix of what you love to do and what you have to do isn't optimal, what action should you take? First, perform your less-favorite elements of your job brilliantly. Your credibility with leaders and teammates will increase when you can be counted on to get even the most mundane tasks done effectively. Few people want to work with a prima donna who believes they are too good for some tasks, and "we all need to do windows." While you're doing great work, you can also communicate with your leader about what you love and your longer-term goals so you're developing in the direction you want to grow.

In addition, if you find the proportions of what you love to do and what you have to do aren't right, you could seek another role or ask to be reassigned. You could also work with teammates to explore whether any adjustments could be made. Perhaps your colleague loves to do what you don't and could take on more of that type of work.

Overall, the solution is to be conscious and intentional about your work so you can make choices and empower yourself about your short- and long-term opportunities. When you're realistic about the mix of your job—and the less exciting tasks it may include—you'll find that doing work you love is 100 percent possible, and it will help you cultivate joy.

► **REFLECT**

To what extent is the mix of your work right for you?

_____

_____

_____

_____

_____

_____

_____

_____

_____

_____

_____

_____

_____

_____

_____

_____

_____

_____

_____

_____

## Healthy Cultures

Beyond consideration for your company and your job, you can also give thought to the health of your organization's culture. There has been a lot of press lately on toxicity—toxic cultures, bosses, or coworkers.

A poll by FlexJobs found that 84 percent of people have worked with a toxic coworker, and 87 percent have worked with a toxic boss. But what's the difference between true toxicity and hard work or high pressure? It's worth being specific about your experiences, because it's possible to go fast, press hard, and feel high expectations within a culture that also embraces well-being and respect for employees.

In fact, a significant number of people are reporting they are busier than they've ever been. Just when they feel like they can't go any faster, something else is added to their plate. Or just when they have solved the biggest problem ever, they are faced with an even more difficult situation. So what's the difference between heavy pressure and toxic pressure, or the difference between intense burdens and toxic burdens?

When you're differentiating between busy and toxic, here are ways to view the experience.

**Your work is appreciated** or **Too much is never enough.** In a healthy situation, your work is valued. You may not hear it every day, but you know your boss and colleagues appreciate what you do. They may communicate your work matters in small ways through a thumbs-up or a quick "Thank you." Their gratefulness doesn't have to be communicated with fanfare or neon lights, but you know how they feel. In a toxic environment, your work never seems to be enough. You can climb a figurative Mount Everest, and your boss will judge you for being winded and direct you to the next peak. Or you can walk on water, and your coworkers will fault you for not being able to swim and point you to the next ocean of responsibility.

**Your work is connected to the big picture** or **You're in the dark about priorities.** In a positive work experience, you can see how your work is tied to something beyond yourself. You know your tasks are necessary for a colleague's project upstream, or you see how your work links to your internal or external customer. In a less positive experience, your work is disconnected, and you struggle to see how it's being used. In top-secret, high-security operations, each person is only able to see their own small slice of work. But if you're not part of a highly sensitive security effort, being kept in the dark can be a symptom of toxicity. Mateo told a story of being a spokesperson for his company's new marketing platform. He regularly recorded audio and video supporting the campaign but was never allowed to see the final spots that ran on local stations (unless he happened to catch them when and where they were broadcast).

**Your ideas matter** or **You are muted.** In positive organizational cultures, you can speak up, share your ideas, and feel like people are listening. Not all your input will be brilliant, and not all your suggestions will be adopted, but your team will give everyone the opportunity for appropriate amounts of influence. In a toxic culture, you may be shut down, or your ideas may be discounted. Janiyah shared how she would speak up with an idea in a meeting and be ignored. A few minutes later, a favored coworker would put forward the same idea and receive positive feedback. This happened repeatedly, and others began to notice. Ultimately, she left the toxic environment and found another job.

**The meetings are about the work** or **There is always a hidden agenda.** In healthy environments, you'll collaborate with colleagues on the work itself. You'll put your heads together to solve problems or develop new ideas. In a toxic environment, meetings will be packed with hidden agendas, and when people share ideas, there will be winners and losers. You'll have a palpable sense of competition for airtime and favor, taking up a lot of emotional energy. No environment is totally without politics, but in a toxic environment, it takes center stage and distracts from the work.

**Feedback is open and constructive** or **Things are handled through back channels.** When companies are effective, they focus on improvement. You'll receive feedback on your work and also on your impact so you can learn, adjust, and improve. In a toxic culture, you may not receive feedback at all. Unhealthy cultures are rife with behind-your-back conversations or efforts to undermine others. In addition, healthy cultures will provide feedback about your tasks or your approach. Toxic cultures tend to make things personal. DeAndre said at his company, when new people joined, it was like they received an invisible pile of chips (think: Vegas). Chips would be added or taken away without someone's knowledge. When they were out of chips, they were fired.

**Work is distributed equitably** or **Things never seem fair.** There will always be ebbs and flows in the work, and sometimes you'll be busier than your colleagues and vice versa. This is natural. But in a toxic culture, work never seems to be distributed fairly. You may see some people breaking their backs while others coast. When this becomes a chronic trend, it may be a symptom of toxicity.

**People are imperfect** or **Behavior is bad.** In a healthy culture, your colleagues will have plenty of imperfections (as do you). But in a toxic culture, there will be a lot of bad behavior (think: lying, cheating, and the like). In addition, when your work experience is positive, you'll laugh with your colleagues—even if it's gallows humor—while you're all struggling through a tough project. In a toxic situation, you'll only want to cry.

**You have small setbacks** or **You see unavoidable patterns**. No company is perfect, and you may experience a few of these challenges. In a toxic culture, however, you'll experience a significant number of these dynamics over time. It's a matter of degree and frequency. You can overlook mistakes and small struggles, but a long-standing pattern is cause for concern.

Being busy can be exhausting, but that isn't necessarily bad if you know your work matters and experience respect and camaraderie. You'll have busy periods, but you know those will give way to more reasonable workloads. On the other hand, toxic work experiences represent the extreme—places where you may wither and from which you'll want (and need) to escape.

If you're in a tough situation, give it your best, be optimistic, and do all you can to make things work. Give your coworkers and your employer the benefit of the doubt. But then if things still seem toxic, face reality, gather your courage, and harness your energy to make new choices and find brighter horizons.

▶ REFLECT

In what ways do you experience high expectations in your work?

_____

_____

_____

_____

## HAPPINESS IN PRACTICE

► Diego was unhappy with his company's culture. He didn't feel like it was a good match to his values. He reflected on his dissatisfaction and also on the strong relationships he had built with his colleagues. He also considered his influence and realized he had a lot of pull in the organization. Despite his frustrations, he decided to stay with the organization. He advocated for better policies and systems and also consistently demonstrated his character and integrity. Over time, he was able to see the difference he was making within his team and his department.

## HAPPINESS IN ACTION

► Be selective about the organization you work for, making the best match between your job, your skills, and your desires.
► Make a commitment to doing your best, even when work isn't ideal.
► Be realistic, knowing no job is perfect.

# 4

# CHOOSING RELATIONSHIPS

Connections with coworkers and colleagues create joy. However, despite being more connected than ever, we may be experiencing less fulfillment. This is the importance of trust, empathy, and the balance of working alone and with others.

## Loneliness and Social Media

You've built your following on LinkedIn, you have more friends than the average person on Facebook, and you're known for never breaking a streak on Snapchat. So why do you still feel disconnected?

Social media can be bad for your health. It makes you feel connected—even though you're actually not—and it contributes to depression and negative comparisons. It's hard to break away though, since we're so connected. What's the alternative?

First, it's important to know not all social media is bad. Social media can be a terrific way to extend your network, stay in touch with Grandma, and share photos of your new puppy with people who share your interest in her. What is a bit out of control for many of us is our use of social media. The solution isn't to ditch social media or devices entirely but to manage ourselves and our use of them.

If you are using social media to feel more connected, a recent study published in the *American Journal of Health Promotion* suggests it may not be working. Positive interactions on social media didn't help people feel happier, and negative interactions magnified feelings of sadness. It seems that social media doesn't always have positive effects. It can have negative effects instead.

Another study published in *Psychology of Popular Media* showed comparing yourself to others via social media also has negative effects, leading to brooding and symptoms of depression. As the saying goes, "Comparison is the thief of joy."

## YOU CAN'T REALLY BE THAT CONNECTED

Dunbar's number is a fascinating concept to apply here. Robin Dunbar developed the idea that based on our brain size, 150 is the maximum number of meaningful connections with others any person can have. This is the number of people you can reasonably keep up with—knowing enough about them to ask about their family or their new house. Another way to think of it: this is how many people you could run into at a restaurant and join informally for a bite to eat without feeling like you were intruding. The interesting thing about social media is our connections have increased, but only in our outer circles of acquaintances. We may have eight hundred friends on Facebook, but they are not people we know well or whom we might call if we had a flat tire. Your LinkedIn connections may be vast, but many are only more distant contacts, and you may not even recognize them if you ran into them out of context—at the grocery store for example—rather than in a business setting.

## NOTHING BEATS FACE-TO-FACE

Social media use also has an opportunity cost. Susan Pinker, in her book *The Village Effect*, demonstrated that face-to-face interactions are best for our happiness, physical health, and mental well-being. Unfortunately, if we're prioritizing time Snapchatting our friends or posting photos on Instagram, we're not truly connecting. Or even if we are in person, we may be heads-down on a device rather than interacting with the people around us.

Hence our loneliness. We are more "connected" than ever,

but the number of close connections we have hasn't changed, and we're lacking true face-to-face human relationships.

What's the alternative? How should you manage your social media usage? Here are a few suggestions.

**Know your stats.** While it may be disheartening, pay attention to your metrics. Use your device's tracking to be aware of how much you're using it, what you're using it for, and how often you're tied to it. Knowing your usage is the first step toward managing it. Ironically, there are apps for this if you need help, especially at first, in establishing more control.

**Get away from your device.** As tough as it might be, turn off and tune in to the world around you. Take a walk, get out into nature, have coffee with a friend, and meet face-to-face with others. If you do have your device with you, keep it out of sight. One study from researchers at the University of Texas at Austin showed that even having your device in sight reduces cognitive capacity and distracts you and others.

**Be in charge of your device rather than letting it be in charge of you.** Just because it rings or vibrates does not mean you must respond to your device. Remind yourself that you're in charge, not your device or the people on the other end of it who have just pinged you.

**Use your device as a relationship builder.** When you're in a conversation where a fun fact comes up, check your device for the information you need, use your app to find your friends, and make your dinner reservation so you can get right into your favorite restaurant. Bottom line: use your device to facilitate relationships rather than as a barrier to connecting.

**Prioritize people.** Nothing is more important than your relationships. Whether you're an introvert or an extrovert, you need time by yourself as well as real human connections with others. Solitary confinement is one of the worst punishments a society imposes because it's so painful. Avoid creating your own isolation. Instead, give priority to people. When you're talking with others, make eye contact, invest, and be present in the conversation. You'll be better for it, and so will they.

► REFLECT

In what ways has social media shifted your interactions or your relationships?

_____

_____

_____

_____

_____

_____

_____

# Empathy

Empathy sometimes gets a bad rap as a soft skill that is too fluffy to matter in business. But in reality, it can be the pathway to hard results.

First, it's important to know empathy is a capability we all have, allowing us to put ourselves in the place of another person and experience their feelings. We all crave connectedness, and it seems our brains are hard-wired to mirror others' experiences. Research published in *Child Development* shows that children as young as two demonstrate understanding that others have perspectives that are different from their own.

There are important benefits of empathy.

- **Identity.** Empathy affects our own identity. We tend to understand ourselves through the people we spend time with, and we derive our sense of self from the types of people with whom we have the closest relationships.

- **Cooperation.** Empathy also facilitates cooperation, which is critical for teams to function effectively. When empathy is introduced into decision-making, it increases cooperation and even causes people to be more empathetic. Empathy fosters more empathy.

- **Innovation.** Empathy can expand your horizons and extend your thinking. By understanding an unfamiliar point of view, you can stretch and test new perspectives and ideas—a key process for successful innovation and ensuring your thinking doesn't stagnate.

► **Influence.** In addition to the benefits of empathy to the community, empathy is also good for you individually because it can help you persuade and influence others. Putting yourself in others' shoes and understanding their perspectives facilitates discussion. Empathy also allows you to use their perspectives as a common starting point toward influencing them to your point of view.

## EMPATHY AND ACTION

There are two ways to empathize. You can empathize by considering someone else's thoughts ("If I were in his/her position, what would I be thinking right now?"), which is known as cognitive empathy. You can also focus on another person's feelings ("Being in his/her position would make me feel ____"), which is known as emotional empathy. Of course, the gold standard for considering others' perspectives is to ask them about it directly, but short of that, it is helpful to imagine what they must be going through. Ultimately, both cognitive and emotional empathy benefit identity, influence, cooperation, and expanded thinking.

It is considering a team member's perspectives and making

a new recommendation that helps achieve greater success for the group. Use empathy to sell ideas, connect with colleagues, accomplish more in a team, expand your own perspectives, and cultivate joy.

## CLARIFYING EMPATHY

It's important to start with clarity about empathy—that it has tremendous benefits that have been proven for people and for businesses. From greater innovation and better leadership to increased engagement and work satisfaction, there is plenty to celebrate.

True empathy is feeling what another person feels. It is experiencing distress along with a coworker who is going through a hard time or feeling uncertain along with a colleague who is making a critical career decision. But empathy isn't the same as caring, compassion, or kindness.

It is totally possible to feel caring toward someone and to express compassion or kindness without literally feeling their distress—to *feel for* rather than *feel as* someone else is feeling. Of course, caring and compassion and kindness are fundamental to healthy individuals, relationships, and communities.

## CAUTION WITH EMPATHY

As you're expressing empathy, you'll want to ensure you're both kind and appropriately cautious. Perhaps surprisingly, it's possible for empathy to go too far or for it to motivate the wrong kinds of actions and decisions. The key is to get the balance right, with plenty of empathy at the right times but not so much that it damages you or others.

## TOO MUCH OF A GOOD THING

Too much empathy can be too much. Here's why.

**You'll burn out.** One of the biggest reasons to manage your empathy is to ensure you don't experience burnout. It would be tough to overdo kindness or compassion, but when you feel deeply for others, it can put a tremendous amount of stress on you. Experiencing your own tension as well as the pain, anxiety, or trauma of others can be extreme. And it can compromise your own health and degrade your ability to give. Give thought to what people are going through (called perspective taking), and pay attention to their challenges, but try not to take on their pain. Take action, reach out, and help but without owning their pressures or turmoil. These approaches will protect your well-being so you have the energy to continue being compassionate toward both yourself and others.

**You'll make poor decisions.** An interesting series of studies found that too much empathy can get in the way of making decisions that take enough data into account, causing you to focus too much in one direction and leave out important additional information. For example, volunteers who heard about one person in need tended to want to help that person at the expense of others who were also in need. In addition, when you feel connected with others, the brain chemical oxytocin can make you especially loyal to them. This is generally a good thing, but it can also make you distrustful and exclusionary toward those whom you perceive to be different or removed from your inner circle, setting up the conditions for bias or unfairness. Learn about situations that matter to you, and nurture your connections with others, but also seek plenty of information about contexts and conditions outside one person or a small group of people so you can make decisions that are good for the whole of a community and that are informed by broad perspective and knowledge. Continue caring for your people—and those who are closest—but also reach out to those who are different from you, and get to know people outside your inner circle so you can be more generous and open-minded toward those who may be less familiar to you.

**You'll be less effective.** Another side effect of too much empathy is losing focus on all the other things that are also important. Great teammates are empathetic, but they also provide new ideas, challenge the status quo, and contribute their unique skills to a project. Great leaders are empathetic, but they also motivate vision and purpose, they hold people accountable, and they provide growth opportunities. Embrace empathy, but also ensure you don't overfocus to the exclusion of other important ways to bring your best. Identify how you can be most successful in your role. Prioritize the top five areas on which you want to focus—including empathy—and then ensure you're putting effort toward the attributes that mean the most to you.

## IN PRAISE OF KINDNESS

While too much empathy can have damaging effects, acting with kindness, care, and compassion toward others is a very good thing. When you put energy toward others and their welfare, of course you're doing good things for the community. But in addition, you tend to be happier and more engaged and have a greater sense of self-esteem as well. This is because humans have an instinct to matter and contribute to the community.

When you volunteer at the food bank with your team, it's great for the community, and you're also building positive relationships with others. When you offer to help a colleague who is struggling with a project, you're aiding in her success, but you're also building your own skills. The most sustainable communities are those in which individual needs are met and group needs are met as well and where there is a terrific sense of satisfaction and harmony for both.

Keep demonstrating empathy, but manage it as well so you don't burn out, make suboptimal decisions, or lose focus.

Continue being compassionate, and take ongoing action to contribute toward the group, knowing these are very good for you and your happiness and also positive for the community as a whole.

▶ **REFLECT**

In what ways have you demonstrated empathy toward others?

# Working Alone

Popular wisdom tells us collaborating is the best way to work and the pathway to the greatest amount of joy at work, but is that true all the time? No.

While work is fundamentally social and teamwork is critical to any positive work experience, it shouldn't be the only way you work. Whether you're an introvert or an extrovert, you need time with others and time alone. In fact, being together all the time can actually get in the way of effectiveness.

Embracing alone time can be very good for mental well-being and performance, according to a study in the journal *Motivation and Emotion*. Appreciating time to reflect, solving problems on your own, and asserting independence are important life skills.

Productivity may also be enhanced by working alone. Researchers at the University of Calgary found that when people around you are working slowly, it may degrade your own productivity. Therefore, working at your own productive pace can be the best approach for the greatest effectiveness.

## HOW TO CREATE MORE TIME ALONE

Time alone is valuable for many reasons, but creating it can be a challenge. Here are ways to find (or create!) time alone.

**First, distinguish between loneliness and being alone.** Our society tends to overvalue social time and undervalue alone time. So remind yourself how time alone is valuable for reflecting, rejuvenating, and being mindful. Remind yourself of the value of being alone.

**Set boundaries.** If your Saturday lunch with a friend always goes long, set a time limit so you have the opportunity for a solitary walk in the park on your way home. Or if a phone call from your aunt tends to go on and on, explain at the beginning of the conversation that you only have a limited amount of time because you have other obligations (to yourself).

**Use your in-between times.** Rather than opening Instagram or Facebook while you're waiting in line at the pharmacy, and rather than dialing a friend while you're on the subway, take advantage of these moments to be by yourself and in your own mind without the clutter of others.

**Revel in the solitary.** Figure out what you love to do, and find ways to spend time with yourself (or with a pet). Plan for the walk you'll take with your dog, learn to kayak on quiet waters, or leverage your Audible subscription—anything to be on your own now and then.

Teamwork works—there is no question. But you must have time alone to be your best and cultivate joy and happiness. Value time with yourself, and plan for it intentionally. You'll be better with others when you're also able to be by yourself.

▶ **REFLECT**

How important is time alone for you?

# Working Together

We all need time alone as well as time with others, and you've known that having good work friends can help you be more satisfied and stay at your job longer. But having great work relationships is also critical to cultivating joy, mental health, and overall well-being. Friends help you gain perspective, tap into self-control, and offer your best—at work and in your community.

This is the power of partnerships and being in a context where cooperation is valued. I've said before that work is fundamentally social, and it is a rare job that doesn't require high amounts of collaboration. In addition, we know from *Vital Friends* by Tom Rath that having a best friend at work is a primary reason people choose to stay with an organization.

So if cooperation, collegiality, and friendship are so important for success through work, how can you build powerful friendships in the work experience?

**Seek out tasks.** One of the most powerful ways to build relationships at work is...well...through the work. While team building is a nice-to-have, winning the three-legged race with a colleague isn't the best way to cement a bond. Working on a tough project together, collaborating on a challenging topic, or working together on a difficult customer issue is much more likely to ensure long-lasting connection.

**Avoid competing.** While competition is seemingly part of all kinds of work, it can be more impactful to find ways to cooperate internally and ensure competition is turned outside the organization. Working together to beat the competition or create new innovations that will help your business recover after an economic downturn will win the day and will make your time with colleagues more rewarding.

**Help others get ahead.** Do your best work so others can do theirs. Follow up, follow through, and be responsive to others around you so they can in turn do good work. Compassion toward people at work will help remove friction when there are so many other, non-work-related challenges all of us must face.

**Be real.** Sometimes, the best support is a colleague who can realize how tough something is and validate you. In a study by researchers at Drexel University related to weight loss, people were able to lose more weight when they were reminded how difficult the task was. This type of approach had a greater positive impact than simply encouraging or cheerleading ("You can do it"). It seems having someone put a name to your reality and reinforce your experience can have a positive effect.

**Listen.** New research from Wake Forest University found that people's cortisol levels, a measure of their stress, were positively affected when they were supported by a partner who listened and acknowledged their feelings. This kind of support is known as "safe-haven support." Look for the kinds of relationships where there is time for camaraderie and empathy in addition to the requisite problem solving needed for the work.

**Offer challenging perspectives.** In addition to building relationships where there is safe-haven support, also seek relationships with support that challenges you. In order to do our best, we need friends who will be brutally honest and point out where we can do better. These are the friends who will tell you that you have the figurative spinach in your teeth. Team members who can help you correct a less-than-helpful trait and become better are the friends who will help you succeed in the long term.

► REFLECT

What do you enjoy about working with others?

_____

_____

_____

_____

_____

_____

_____

_____

_____

# Increasing Your Influence

In addition to building your friendships and relationships, you may also want to increase your influence. It's a great idea, because it can help you advance your career, sell your ideas, improve your results, and enhance your happiness.

Influence is related to happiness because it helps you get more of what you want and it helps you support your community as well.

## THE NATURE OF INFLUENCE

Influence is relevant for every job and every role. It's making your case effectively or persuading someone to your point of view. It's having the ability to effect change. It's building strong, authentic, and trusting relationships that are based on mutual respect that will serve you and others.

Your influence is greatest when people trust you, when they perceive you to have their best interests in mind, and when they sense they have things in common with you. And influence isn't the same as manipulation or coercion. In these cases, you're trying to control or trick someone or even to bully them into doing what you want, which may not be best for them. On the other hand, with positive influence, you're sharing your views and respecting others, and in turn, they're making their own decisions to support you, your ideas, or your direction.

A significant part of influence is the perception of proximity. People tend to build the strongest relationships with those they see most often and get to know best, so many of the approaches for influence are based on creating a sense of proximity—both face-to-face and from a distance.

When you're working at a distance—even some of the time—communication is different, of course. It's harder to interpret intent accurately, it's tougher to build trust and strong bonds, and it requires more effort.

As a result of all this, there are five primary considerations for reimagining relationships for greater influence.

## COMMITMENT

One of the first ways to build strong relationships and increase your influence is through commitment to a relationship. True friendship takes time, but even if you're not seeking a BFF, you'll need to be intentional about how you invest.

Stay in touch with your contacts. Invite them for coffee or lunch or a one-on-one. Get together when they're in town. Reach out and share articles or ideas you know will interest them.

Also consider reciprocity. The strongest relationships— both personal and professional—include back-and-forth exchanges. When you have a relationship with someone and they initiate connections, be sure you do as well, or they will get a strong message you don't value time together. Also consider the ways you share information.

Trust is also built with reciprocity in terms of your sharing. You open up about something, and then they do in turn. This kind of sharing over time tends to build trust, and transparency is the fuel for a trusting relationship.

You can also demonstrate commitment through your attention. With everything coming at people today, distraction is the norm. But by giving your attention, you build your influence. When you're together with someone on the phone, on video, or in person, be fully attentive. Put away your devices, and don't multitask. Instead, when you're truly present, you're demonstrating you value a person and your relationship with them.

When you make a commitment to a relationship, stay in touch, and invest time, you also demonstrate authenticity. You're not just trying to achieve a quick hit of selling something or racking up your number of LinkedIn connections. Instead, you're demonstrating your genuine interest in a relationship.

Know that your network isn't just a game of numbers. You may have thousands of contacts on your social platforms, but you also need people you can call when you need help, who will aid you in a business relationship, who will advocate for you or support you. These kinds of relationships are created with a meaningful level of commitment.

## CONSISTENCY

Another part of building relationships and your influence is consistency. You'll want to commit to making the effort and investing time but also in making the investment regularly. Your influence will be greatest when you play the long game and maintain connections over time. Rather than being a flash in the pan, you'll want to check in routinely.

Consistency is also about how you show up. People prefer others who are predictable—who behave consistently over time. As an example, research has demonstrated that people prefer a poor leader who is consistent rather than a leader who is inconsistent—kind or attentive one day and aloof or demeaning the next. People don't trust what they don't understand, and consistency is a large measure of how people grow accustomed to who you are and how you relate to them.

The cognitive bias of recency also plays a role here. People tend to keep top of mind what has just happened, and things that have occurred further in the past are further from awareness, so you build relationships by staying in touch regularly and therefore staying in recent memory.

Another relevant cognitive bias is a familiarity bias in which people tend to have greater acceptance for those who are more familiar to them, and they are more influenced by them as well. This points to the concept of cadence: strive to see people with regularity. Perhaps you want to see someone at least once a month or once a quarter. For professional or sales relationships, in particular, you might plan for check-ins so you don't lose track of someone in the crush of so much to do and so little time. Prioritize relationships, and plan for a cadence of contact.

## CURIOSITY

Curiosity is also a foundation for great relationships, and it's the basis for empathy as well. When you're curious, you're genuinely interested in someone else's point of view. And you're humble—knowing your opinion isn't the only one and that others will have important perspectives based on their unique experiences.

Likability is also a key element of influence. When people like you, you'll be more persuasive, and your likability comes in part from how you make people feel. In fact, research has demonstrated people's view of you is often based more on how you make them feel about themselves than how they feel about you. Or, said differently, how they feel about you is based on how you cause them to feel about themselves. Curiosity works for you, because you learn and grow and connect, but it also works for others because it reinforces their feeling that you value them.

Interestingly, curiosity, humility, and fallibility are also linked with credibility. You need to establish competence and expertise, but then you enhance credibility by being open about what you don't know and about where you wonder. Once you've demonstrated a level of knowledge, you are wise to communicate that you don't know everything and that you also have areas where you seek input and differences of opinion.

When you're curious, you're sending a message that you value others' views and that you're open to learning from them.

## CONTINUITY

Continuity is also important to relationships and influence. Continuity is constancy over time—cycles of contact and meaning that continue beyond a quick one time contact.

Think about electricity, in which continuity represents a closed circuit or a complete flow. When you're building relationships and increasing your influence, give thought to how well you follow up and follow through.

Responsiveness, accessibility, and follow-through are strongly related to influence. You don't need to be available twenty-four seven, but you'll want to get back to people quickly and be accessible through various channels.

## COLLECTIVITY

Another way to influence is through your teamwork with others.

Statistically, people are more likely to be influenced by you when you're associated with someone they already know or when you've been recommended by someone they know. "A friend of a friend" is apt—people are more likely to trust those whom their friends also trust. Given this, ask others to introduce you if you're seeking to build a new relationship. And nurture your network by doing the same for your contacts.

As you're building influence, also manage relationships among teams. In sociological terms, you can compare a dirt path of relationships to superhighways. With a dirt path, you might have a relationship with one other person. You walk a small dirt path back and forth in your ongoing relationship with each other.

But a more powerful level of influence is built with super-highways in which you and members of your team have plenty of relationships across departments and with multiple others across organizations. You have a lot of touch points among many people, enhancing influence for the whole group. You positively embed and entangle within a team, department, or organization.

## PERCEIVED PROXIMITY

The Latin roots of the word *influence* are "to flow into," so you can think of building your influence by maintaining ongoing, two-way flows in your relationships that persist over time.

Consider increasing your influence with both intent and intentionality. Your intent is for genuine, authentic relationships, and you'll be intentional about how you invest time, effort, and attention in relationships, resulting in terrific influence and all the benefits that arise from it.

► **REFLECT**

In what ways do you influence others?

_____

_____

_____

_____

_____

_____

_____

_____

_____

_____

_____

_____

_____

_____

_____

# Building Trust

Of course, your influence will be greatest when you build trust. And trust is a primary ingredient for the most rewarding and joyful relationships. In a trusting relationship, you know you can rely on a person, and you believe in their integrity. You trust them to do the right thing and have your best interests at heart.

## TASK AND RELATIONSHIP TRUST

You can think of trust in terms of both task and relationship interactions. When you trust someone will follow through on a task, you have task trust, and when you trust they will keep your confidences, you have relationship trust. And it's possible to have one and not the other.

In a creative example, the difference between task and relationship trust has been compared to pizza and your dog. If you have task trust, you trust someone to show up responsibly to care for your dog while you're away, and if you have relationship trust, you're happy to share a pizza and deep conversation with someone.

In a more serious example, you may have a colleague who is impeccable with follow-through but isn't someone you would confide in about your career goals, or you work with a teammate who knows all your biggest secrets but is terrible at getting things done. Of course, the best relationships are those where you have high levels of both task and relationship trust.

## BIG BENEFITS

Trust has big payoffs. When you feel a high degree of trust in your teammate, your leader, or your team, you're more likely to feel a sense of psychological safety and bring your full self to your work.

You'll expose your goofy sense of humor, your unexpected ideas, or the eccentric quality that makes you unique—all very good for your well-being and also for the strength the team can derive from tapping into plenty of diverse perspectives and talents.

And ironically, when you feel most comfortable in relationships, you can embrace higher levels of discomfort—or positive stretch—in your learning, development, and innovative processes. You feel emotionally safe taking appropriate risks and trying new things in your work. You feel protected enough to push toward new innovations or test your limits as you develop new skills.

## BUILDING TRUST

According to a new study by researchers at Ohio State University and to years of additional study on what it takes to build trust, you can take a few key actions to create and sustain trust. When you do, the people around you will tend to feel more comfortable and share more openly. They'll also tend to feel more valued, confident, and empowered, and they'll be more likely to take positive action.

**Admit mistakes**. In the study, those who were able to view themselves accurately and admit their own mistakes tended to foster trust in others. When you're more vulnerable—sharing your own concerns or uncertainties—you tend to develop more trusting relationships.

**Appreciate others.** Based on the research, another important component of creating feelings of trust was valuing others and their strengths. The best colleagues not only recognize and express their appreciation for others, they also value relationships for the long term and demonstrate they care by seeking to help others. They tune in, ask questions, listen, and show empathy and compassion.

**Be open to learning.** A third component of the study on expanding trust was an openness to learning from others—distinguished from an arrogance or belief in having all the answers. Intellectual humility reinforces this approach. People tend to build credibility by holding clear opinions and expertise and balancing these with a willingness to listen to multiple points of view and learn from others who think differently.

**Be honest.** Of course.

**Honor commitments.** People want to work with others who follow through and follow up and who can be counted on.

When you meet your commitments, others can be more successful in their roles, and this applies to commitments both big and small.

**Stand up for what's right.** A study of sixty different societies by the University of Oxford found that a fundamental need of all those studied was a perception of fairness. In addition, when people don't perceive they are being treated fairly, they are more likely to leave a job, a leader, or an organization. So in building trust, you can stand up for what's right and take action to ensure practice is in alignment with values. You can take a stand on key issues and go to bat for a coworker who needs your support or advocacy.

Building trust is no small challenge today, but it never has been. And taking action to intentionally build trust is worth the effort, because it will create more fulfilled, joyful relationships for you and for others.

▸ REFLECT

In which of your relationships do you have the greatest levels of trust?

_____

_____

_____

_____

## HAPPINESS IN PRACTICE

► Soren was struggling with feelings of loneliness and depression. He realized he was spending significant hours online but feeling more disconnected than ever. He was also becoming cynical about the world and his future. When he tuned in to the news, it always seemed to be bad. Soren decided to limit his time on social media, and he also worked on consuming less media as well. When he felt tempted to be on his device, Soren took a walk or sat near the river instead. Over time, Soren not only felt better but also started a walking group with others who were seeking to be outside more frequently.

## HAPPINESS IN ACTION

► Manage your social media consumption so it doesn't consume you.

► Balance opportunities to be face-to-face with others as well as alone so you can recharge in the ways that work best for you.

► Consider others' experiences, imagine what they may be experiencing, and offer support and compassion.

# 5

# CHOOSING GROWTH

A growth mindset and an emphasis on learning contribute to joy. Saying yes, learning from failure, and embracing stress can also be strong contributors to a joyful life.

## Saying Yes

In the work-life discussion, we spend a lot of time talking about having appropriate boundaries and knowing how to say no. However, you may want to delicately decline less often and just say yes more of the time, because yes is the fastest route to developing your talents, growing your career, and cultivating joy.

Of course, boundaries are important, and you have to be able to appropriately disengage and set limits on your work (more on that in a later chapter). But you don't want to inadvertently set limits on *yourself* by taking a too-stringent approach to new opportunities.

When you stretch, you tend to be more stimulated and satisfied in your work. When you can do a job without thinking about it, things can become too routine, and you risk burnout. In fact, a challenge and the unknown ("How should I handle this situation?") can be very motivating. In addition, saying yes increases the likelihood that you can fully contribute your gifts and skills and find meaning in your work.

Saying yes is all about trust.

**Trust yourself.** You should always be learning, developing, and nurturing your talents. When new opportunities come up or you're invited to take on that new project, trust yourself and your skills. Know your limitations so you don't say yes to the wrong things. But also trust your capabilities and the work you've done to prepare for the next chapter.

**Trust others.** When you're offered the opportunity to take on more responsibility, trust the people who have assessed you so positively. Sometimes, we can be our own harshest critics, and it can be helpful to be more gentle. See yourself through the optimistic lens others have on you. When you say yes to a stretch opportunity, ask what it is the person has seen in you, and ask for support as you take on that next role. Trust that others are seeing legitimate talent within you and will help you be successful.

**Trust the timing.** You can't always know whether the timing for a new opportunity is perfectly right, because life always includes a lot of other variables. If you take that promotion, how will it affect your availability for your relationships with partners or friends? How might it impact the energy you have for your family or hobbies? My advice: give it a try. When you do new things, you'll have to invest time and effort, but you'll also find that overall, you're more energized by the challenge and therefore actually have more time and capacity to give for the other important parts of your life.

So which opportunities will be the most fruitful when you're saying yes?

Give your enthusiastic thumbs-up to opportunities that allow you to build on existing skills. The ideal situation lets you apply what you already know and have elements of easy success while also stretching you into new areas. Moving from HR to finance if you've never seen a spreadsheet may not be very wise, but moving from HR to strategy could be a natural fit, given the importance of talent for an organization's future.

Prioritize options that let you meet new people and broaden your network. The connections you make are deeply rewarding because belonging is essential to well-being. In addition, building your network helps you over the long run so you can learn from others and grow your relationships.

One caveat: when you say yes, you may not always be *paid* for the stretch you're making. Say yes when you believe you'll be noticed and ultimately compensated; just don't expect every new opportunity will come with an increase in pay. It's fair for your company to ask you to try a new role or expand your scope in order to give you a chance to learn and grow without paying you for each new task on your list. Take the leap. Giving discretionary effort and going above and beyond shouldn't go unnoticed, and you'll be rewarded over time.

Saying yes to opportunities is about helping the company. But even more importantly, it's about saying yes to yourself. Say yes more than you say no in order to validate your skills, develop your talents, and find motivation through new challenges. Trusting yourself may be the best reward of all.

► REFLECT

What is something you've said yes to?

_____

_____

_____

_____

_____

# Learning from Failure

When you say yes more, you may also fail more. Failure is legitimately connected with success though. While most research is judicious in saying it makes (only) correlations between data, a new Northwestern University study found *causal* connections between failure and success. In researching 1,184 grant applications with the National Institutes of Health, it found that those who stuck it out after failure ultimately had a higher likelihood of success. While a small percentage dropped out after failing to receive funding, those who stayed the course after a failure saw a 6 percent increase in success.

So it really is true. If you can keep going after you fail—never giving up—you'll be more likely to succeed in the end. As Thomas Edison said, "Many of life's failures are people who did not realize how close they were to success when they gave up." If at first you don't succeed, try, try again.

## FAILURE IS MESSY

Despite the lofty notions about failure and its dignity, the truth is it hurts to fail. At best, failure can feel like a waste of time or, at worst, like a personal indictment. Failure can cause you to regroup, retrench, or retreat.

It can cost money and time (the new suit you bought for the interview or the move you made to the city for the job that didn't last). It can cause you to course correct (the meeting went sideways, and you need to rethink the project, or the certification exam you failed makes you reconsider whether you're really right for that specialty). Most of all, failure can make you question yourself—who you are and what you're good at. This is what makes it messiest of all.

How do you get through the turmoil that can come from failure?

**Remind yourself failure isn't about you as a person.** Rather, it is about a skill or capability you can build. Take a growth mindset in which you don't look at your talents as a stagnant set but as something you can develop, nurture, and strengthen. Changing course is a common response to failure, but if you stick with something and continue trying, it can pay big dividends.

**Accept it.** While there may have been things outside your control and while the process or the system might have worked against you, focus instead on how you had a role to play in your failure. Accept it, and find where you can learn from failure. It's a standard suggestion that you should always seek lessons after a fall. But it's familiar because it's right. Learning from success is less automatic—you may be so busy celebrating and taking steps forward, you forget to reflect. Although failure may be based on unfortunate conditions, it provides you with the opportunity to learn and consider how you can strengthen your game for the next time.

**Share your pain.** Sometimes sharing your challenges can be helpful to building connections. Rather than always putting on a happy face and serving up platitudes, open up to trusted colleagues. They may have advice, and demonstrating vulnerability will build relationships.

**Embrace growth.** It's frustrating to think you may have wasted your time on the job you didn't get or the client you didn't win. You might think of the effort you made as sunk cost. But you'll be miles ahead if you consider the work you did as an investment in yourself. What doesn't break you makes you stronger, another tried and true mantra about failure that's really accurate. If you're doing it right, you'll gain resourcefulness, resilience, and perseverance from failure—all good skills to have and characteristics that will make life more rewarding.

**Focus on the future.** If you fail, you'll want to take a breath, step back, and reflect on your lessons learned, but then be ready to move forward. Make a point to find your next inspiration— from someone else who has failed, from a story that inspires you, or from the next opportunity that motivates you. Keep facing forward. One of my mentors always says, "Run toward the fire," by which he means stay in the game, don't give up, and give the next possibility your all.

▶ **REFLECT**

What is a lesson you've learned from failure?

# Embracing Stress

According to the American Psychological Association (APA), stress in the United States is at one of its highest points ever, and over 60 percent of people are stressed about the future and money. Significantly, 61 percent of Americans are also stressed about their work.

But while we admittedly have plenty to worry about, stress and anxiety may not be all bad. The APA also reports that they serve important psychic and social functions, letting us know when to be alert to danger or when we may need to reconsider our choices or behaviors.

In fact, we may have become overly stressed about stress or too anxious about anxiety. Here's why stress and anxiety can be quite constructive.

**It's a signal of commitment.** If you're feeling stressed, it can be a cue you're committed and care about your performance. Even the speaker who regularly addresses audiences will admit to at least a few butterflies before every presentation. This is an indicator she cares about the audience, cares about doing a good job, and wants to succeed—all good things. Likewise, your stress may be a constructive demonstration of your interest in performing well.

**It's a signal of connection.** Stress also demonstrates a healthy connection with others. None of us works in a vacuum.

Even the solitary writer is developing an article for an audience, and the independent graphic designer is creating for a client. Pressure to succeed in the judgment of others is appropriate. It signals we are part of a broader community and realize the value we bring. If our work didn't matter, we would have no cause for stress. Rather, work that matters to the community matters to us and can therefore result in an anxious—and positive— desire to succeed.

**It's a signal of conscience.** Importantly, anxiety can also be a message that we need to do better. Related to being a part of the larger whole, we are responsible for being conscientious and ethical. If we feel a bit out of balance, it may be a trigger to reevaluate our approach or the impact we're having on others. That sarcastic comment or the less-than-positive email—and the anxious feeling that results—may be good reason to apologize or adjust behaviors in the future.

**It's a signal for change.** Pressure in the form of anxiety can also be a prompt for change. When things aren't working out, it is often necessary to consider a shift. Avoid placing blame on others or the situation, and take the opportunity to effect change. Own the opportunity to change your situation—using stress as a catalyst toward a new approach.

**It's a signal of complacency.** Stress can also be caused by a lack of stimulation. We need enough challenge to stay engaged and mentally involved. It is part of the human condition to become accustomed to characteristics around us. This contributes to cognitive efficiency—we don't have to continually process new information. On the other hand, if we don't experience enough that is new, we can become bored. Eustress is a situation in which you feel positive levels of stress based on staying stimulated. Stress based on boredom can be a good trigger to find opportunities to build new skills or engage in new situations, like taking on the next project or reaching for a stretch promotion.

► REFLECT

When have you used stress as a catalyst for change?

_____

_____

_____

_____

_____

_____

_____

_____

_____

_____

_____

## Rethinking Self-Care

Of course another aspect of managing stress is considering how you're caring for yourself. The narrative about self-care is widespread today—including recommendations for plenty of relaxation, resetting, and time away. Unfortunately, some self-care advice can be its own source of stress when it requires you to add to your list of things to do. Now, while you're getting the end-of-the-year report done and buying gifts, you also need to take time for a massage.

The emphasis on self-care can often be tone-deaf: failing to recognize the lack of control people have over their schedules. Some self-care narratives blame people who are busy. If you would just manage yourself better, the mantra goes, you wouldn't be so stressed.

But life ebbs and flows. During some periods, you may have plenty of time for a lovely stroll through the park, yet during other times, you just may need to buckle down and get things done in order to feel more in charge of your day. By realizing this and by giving yourself permission to be busy during demanding times, you can actually address and reduce the pressures in your life.

Some may define self-care as time for yourself and appointments for pampering. But at its core, true self-care is considering what you need, what energizes you, and how you can expand your well-being physically, emotionally, and cognitively. Based on this definition, it's possible to reimagine self-care with new considerations for how it can truly nurture rather than detract from your experience.

Here are several things to consider when defining what self-care means to you.

**Consider speeding up versus slowing down.** One assumption about self-care is that it's always about relaxing or slowing down. But it's worth reflecting on what works best for you. As you're planning your day, you might take five minutes to meditate in the morning, or you might realize that, for you, activity is more helpful in rebuilding your capacities.

If more is best for you, self-care could include a quick walk between meetings or multitasking by ordering gifts online while watching TV. If your self-care includes action, don't judge yourself. Instead, embrace your full schedule—fit everything into the crevices of the calendar. If you need to speed up, go for it.

**Consider spending time with others versus alone.** Self-care is often defined as time by yourself, and getting away can be a great way to feel centered again. But for some, stress may be best reduced by sharing time with others instead. Invite a colleague to help you solve a tough problem at work, or have a shopping trip with your daughter and your mom, or meet with your book group.

Whatever works best for you, be intentional about whom you spend time with. Research by the Harris Poll found that 57 percent of people say their social networks have become smaller but also more connected over the past couple of years. And 31 percent say they have learned whom they can count on and trust most. Interestingly, 33 percent of respondents realized they didn't want to spend time with friends who didn't add value to their life, and 48 percent dropped friendships that were no longer serving them. These are all healthy parts of true self-care: spending time with people you value and reducing the time you invest with those who may sap your energy. If being with others energizes you, then be selective about how you connect and with whom.

**Consider taking on more versus less.** Another common assumption about self-care is that it's usually best when you decline invitations—for socializing, for volunteering, or for embracing new opportunities at work. You'll have more time for yourself when you decline—according to the prevailing wisdom.

But this too is an oversimplification. In fact, taking on new challenges and empowering yourself to do things that stretch your skills and provide the opportunity to build your network can be energizing. Extending outside your comfort zone and learning new things are often linked with happiness.

So if something sounds interesting, consider taking it on. Manage your time so you don't overextend, but also reflect on which activities could actually provide self-care through the stimulation of new pursuits.

**Consider excellence versus perfection.** Another way to redefine self-care is by recalibrating your standards and reducing perfectionism. Of course, you want to do your best and invest effort in things that matter, but perfectionism can undermine your well-being. Obsessing about making mistakes or holding yourself to impossibly high requirements can be damaging. A study featured in the journal *Psychological Bulletin* found that perfectionism has increased over recent years, and research from York St John University in York, England, has found that when people are more perfectionistic, they tend to be more likely to experience depression, burnout, anxiety, and even death.

Strive to be *your* best, not *the* best. Resist the urge to compare yourself with others, and know that your strengths aren't the same as the strengths of others. Be flexible in your standards. Sometimes, you may have time for perfectly healthy farm-to-table meals, and other times, you may need to spin through the drive-through on the way to soccer practice. You may have some of the most creative ideas for a particular initiative at work, or you may need help on a project requiring a skill set you don't possess.

Know that your capacity to meet the demands of work and life will shift. Be patient with yourself and with others.

**Consider experiences versus things**. Some companies try to sell products under the guise of self-care. However, research has demonstrated that people are happier when they spend money on experiences rather than things and that people have a greater sense of joy when they invest time in others rather than only themselves.

Plus, when people spend time on things they enjoy, they perceive they have more time overall. Still, there may never be enough time to do all that you want. There will always be another fun activity to enjoy, vacation to plan, or opportunity at work. But by realizing you can't do everything, you can be more present and focused on what you choose to spend time on.

Enjoy your staycation, take pleasure in the weekend away, and appreciate the job you're in now rather than always pining for the next big thing. Reduce your bucket list. And when you make choices to spend time with your people or on certain activities, put away your device, reduce distractions, and be fully present.

True self-care empowers you to reflect on how you spend your time and where you get your energy and to make the choices that work best for you. You can find the right amount of stretch and build your capabilities to respond so you can enjoy this season for its busyness and all the next periods that will ebb and flow.

► **REFLECT**

Which kinds of self-care work best for you?

_____

_____

_____

_____

_____

_____

_____

_____

_____

_____

_____

_____

_____

_____

_____

_____

_____

_____

_____

## HAPPINESS IN PRACTICE

▶ Charlotte was laid off from her job and struggled to find another. She felt insecure about her abilities and also embarrassed about having been let go. A friend reminded Charlotte about how many people experience layoff (a majority of people at some time in their lives) and offered to practice with Charlotte so she could explain her layoff in confident terms during interviews. Charlotte also got input from another friend about how she could reflect the employment gap on her résumé. After taking a brief break from her job search, Charlotte reentered the process and applied for a large number of jobs. She landed interviews and, with her newfound confidence, was able to get two different job offers—both of which paid more than her previous role.

## HAPPINESS IN ACTION

▶ Seek challenges and opportunities to stretch.
▶ Acknowledge and learn from failure.
▶ Embrace the positive aspects of stress, and remind yourself how it can give you signals about your own development.

# 6

# CHOOSING SUCCESS

In creating joy, play has a key role in everything from innovation to stress relief, and rejecting hustle culture can also create terrific happiness. It's also important to ensure you're not undermining your own success with perfectionism, self-sabotage, or imposter syndrome.

## Play

Accomplish more, create joy, and increase productivity 20 percent? Who doesn't want that? In a new study, teams that played a collaborative video game together for just forty-five minutes were able to increase their productivity on a task by 20 percent.

Perhaps all those expensive team-building programs or out-landish group retreats are overreaching. Perhaps all you need to build culture and improve performance is a gaming council and some willing colleagues.

But it doesn't have to be about gaming.

The reasons play helps teams and their results and the reasons play is also good for your career growth are well founded. Company cultures that allow for play are better able to tap into the best in their employees, and employees themselves can bring more effectiveness into their work.

Here are four reasons you should play more too.

**Play fosters innovation.** Playfulness is linked to humor, and the distance from "Haha" to "Aha" is short. It is often the fun of the unexpected that leads to the novelty of new ideas and thus innovation. Humor is the result of surprise. We laugh or are entertained when we expect one thing and get something else. This is why puns resonate at young ages and why tricks of illusion still intrigue us. Surprise is the pathway toward creativity as well—combining ideas in new ways and embracing the unexpected to build something that hasn't been done before.

**Play unites team members.** Organized play (versus simply goofing around, which has its own merits) tends to have common goals and simple rules. Common goals are good for teams and their work because they align and unite people. This alignment and focus tend to provide a sense of purpose and "line of sight" in which team members can see how their roles matter and how their efforts contribute to the whole. In addition, the simple rules of play provide for just enough structure to help team members feel a sense of boundary and control over the process they use to reach their goal. In short, it's good to feel like your work matters toward a goal you share with others.

**Play lets us bring more of ourselves to work.** Play also tends to build bonds with other team members. When work is all business, we see one side of our teammates. But as I wrote in *Bring Work to Life by Bringing Life to Work*, there are tremendous benefits when we can bring our full selves to work and when we can get to know others more fully. Even those of us with the most introverted preferences for working and living value our fundamental connections with others, and play is a way to create stronger connections. Through play, we have a new lens on those around us—what entertains them, what motivates them, and what we have in common with them.

**Play helps us blow off steam.** Lately, stress can be tough on us physically, emotionally, and cognitively. On the other hand, research demonstrates that spending time in nonwork pursuits and letting the mind wander are both useful for our overall well-being and effectiveness. Play is an antidote to a high-pressure work environment. It helps people get away from their work temporarily and reduce the intensity of their work demands. This kind of rejuvenation can be especially useful in contributing to well-being, productivity, and joy.

## HOW TO PLAY MORE AND ACHIEVE MORE JOY

From innovation and unity to expressing your talent and reducing stress, the reasons for play are compelling. So how do you embrace play? Here are four recommendations.

**Adopt a playful mindset.** Take yourself less seriously, and strive to have a playful attitude. Seek opportunities to laugh and joke with colleagues. You don't have to throw rubber chickens or tell knock-knock jokes. But you can find ways to bring appropriate humor into work situations. Make it a point to smile and laugh. Bringing positive energy into relationships tends to build trust and connections.

**Make the ordinary more creative.** Seek to incorporate a more playful approach into your ordinary day. If your group is brainstorming and putting ideas on sticky notes (how very ordinary), ask them to use images rather than words. One team I know holds regular meetings where they talk about what went well and less well in the previous work cycle. Each week, a member of the team is responsible for finding a new metaphor for their brainstorm. One week, it was the wind in their sails versus the waves slowing them down. Another week, tailwinds versus headwinds, or gas in their engine compared to potholes in their path. You get the idea. They made the ordinary a bit more fun by thinking about things in a different way. This also made them more productive because they got through tasks more quickly, having more fun in the process.

**Be present.** Part of why play is so engaging is that it tends to occupy all our thoughts in the moment. When you're running for the goal in your neighborhood flag football game or strategizing to win your family card game, it's hard to be distracted by other problems. Use this thinking in your work by staying focused in the present. When you're in a meeting, put away distractions, and keep your attention on the items in front of you. Don't worry about the twelve other tasks on your to-do list. You'll be more effective in the moment—and more productive—with this kind of focus.

**Tap into things that bring you joy.** Play makes us more productive because it energizes and engages us. Consider additional factors that do the same. Bring music into your work environment (headphones are optional based on your team's preferences) so you have a happy beat to your work. I know one team that plays a streaming video of puppies at play in their project space. Take breaks that include nature via a walk outdoors or a quick breath of fresh air. Even if you're in the middle of the city, stepping outside for a deep breath can make a world of

143

difference. One company has adopted a norm of "walking meetings" for those conversations that can occur outside a conference room. Consider how music or nature can help you engage more fully in your work and be more productive.

▶ **REFLECT**

What is an experience in which you felt playful?

_____

_____

_____

_____

_____

_____

_____

_____

_____

_____

_____

_____

_____

_____

_____

# Finding Joy by Rejecting Hustle Culture

Critical to the ability to find joy is the importance of not doing too much. If you subscribe to the culture of busyness, sometimes called hustle culture (and even sporting its own hashtag #hustleculture), you have fallen victim to the always-on, go-without-stopping, busy-is-cool lifestyle.

Sometimes people even use busyness as a signal of status, as the ever-popular response to "How are you?" demonstrates. The reply "I'm so busy!" means we're important. Those who are busy have an indispensable set of skills in high demand. Those with too much to do are highly valued and sought after.

Unfortunately, the opposite seems to be true.

Our cult of busyness is actually undermining our effectiveness and joy despite the social norms to the contrary. It's time to put aside busyness and find ways to disengage.

Businesses seek engagement and lament data that suggests only about one-third of people are actively engaged. But perhaps always-on engagement isn't the best goal in the first place.

There are five good business reasons to break the busyness habit.

**Better thinking.** Constant multitasking is bad for your brain, and it actually makes it difficult to bring deep attention to any work. Focus is what's required for empathy, for problem solving, and for thinking in new ways. The ways we consume information actually change our patterns of perception, causing us to process information more superficially. But when we take breaks and remove ourselves from the constancy of work, we can reprioritize deeper-level processing and the meaning in our work.

**Innovation and confidence.** In our frenetic pace, we've lost the in-between times—the interstitial moments—when our minds can wander. Gone are the minutes in the car when we're just listening to our favorite song or waiting in line at the grocery store and we can just be. We tend to fill these moments with conference calls or the opportunity to catch up on our emails— even for a few seconds. But getting away from work has multiple benefits. In one study conducted at Drexel University, taking the time to do artwork increased participants' self-confidence and belief in their ability to complete their work-related tasks. Another study published in the *Journal of Business and Psychology* found allowing time for the mind to wander resulted in people feeling refreshed and less stressed, leaving them ready to tackle their work anew.

**Better health.** Stress is harmful. But sometimes it's not even the work itself that causes stress; it's the expectation of constant availability and the feeling of being depleted by the demands. We aren't robots, and we can't be at our best when we are always on. We must take breaks. Consider a pilot. On a long flight, the pilot isn't flying the plane in manual mode constantly. Those moments when the plane is flying through a clear, barrier-free sky, autopilot is the best approach. This keeps the pilot fresh for times when their are most necessary—during takeoff, landing, or challenging moments that come up during flight.

**Reasonable expectations.** Another reason to disengage is so your employees and coworkers can as well. It is a common leadership fallacy that managers can shield their employees from too much work by working more themselves. But rather than protecting employees, they set the stage for even more demands to be imposed on the team. In addition, the primary way people learn is by observing others—by social modeling. When leaders or colleagues work extreme hours, they inadvertently send a message to others that they should do the same. By freeing up time, managing boundaries, and having a life, leaders and coworkers set the expectation that these things are not just okay but expected.

**Development of the team.** Finally, disengaging now and then creates the opportunity for others to develop their skills. When a team member is able to get away or take a vacation, it opens the door for others to cover for them. A coworker's vacation can be the perfect opportunity for another team member to step in and stretch their skills to fill the gap. A boss I had early in my career used to say an effective leader could take vacations because he had a capable team who could handle things while he was away. If a leader couldn't take a vacation, it was a reflection that he hadn't adequately developed the team.

► REFLECT

In what ways have you experienced hustle culture?

_____

_____

_____

_____

_____

_____

_____

_____

_____

_____

_____

_____

_____

_____

_____

_____

# Perfectionism

In addition to rejecting hustle culture, you can also avoid perfectionism and avoid letting it get in the way of your progress. Of course, you want to excel at work, and perfection may seem like the best pathway for career growth. But it can be a barrier to your happiness and an obstacle to getting ahead in some surprising ways. It's to your advantage to let go of the pursuit of perfection and find ways to be excellent without being ideal.

If you try to be perfect, you're in good company. A study of over forty-one thousand people published in *Psychological Bulletin* found perfectionism has increased over time, partly because of the comparisons people make with each other on social media and partly because of the competitive environments that colleges and employers are increasingly creating.

Some aspects of perfectionism—setting high standards and working toward goals proactively—can be good for your career, but perfectionism has a significant downside. Obsessing about making mistakes or letting others down or holding yourself to impossibly high standards can have negative consequences.

According to research examining forty-three different studies over twenty years by York St John University, perfectionism is linked to burnout as well as depression, anxiety, and even mortality.

Part of getting out of the perfectionist trap is understanding how it holds you back.

**Perfectionism is demotivating.** By seeking to be perfect, you'll ultimately demotivate yourself. Striving for excellence and pushing yourself are wonderful motivators, but you'll reduce your engagement if you carry these too far. With ideals that are unattainable, you'll never feel like you're good enough, and you'll miss out on the rewards and joys of accomplishment. When you're down or disheartened, it will be tough to put your energy into your work, and you'll detract from your own effectiveness.

You'll get further if you embrace your limits and do your best. With this alternative, you'll be able to invest energy in your responsibilities and relationships, and in turn, people will feel good about working with you (read: your career will benefit).

**Perfectionism distances you from others.** Another drawback of perfectionism is the way it distances you from colleagues. People may not want to work with you because they sense your impossibly high expectations and know they won't measure up. Or they will want to avoid the overwork or overthinking that become your hallmark.

If you fall into the trap of believing you're close to perfect, you also run the risk of intimidating others who know they aren't all that. In addition, if you avoid admitting mistakes, you'll come across as inauthentic. People won't trust you, because they know your Teflon exterior isn't the real you.

Of course, you want to be professional, and you won't share your imperfections with everyone, but you'll also want to achieve the necessary balance where you have the professional courage to express where you need help and where you don't have everything figured out. This authenticity will deepen relationships, build your credibility, and contribute to your happiness.

**Perfectionism reduces your effectiveness.** Another reason perfectionism is a barrier to your career growth is that it reduces your ability to do brilliant work. If you're unable to move ahead or can't get anything done, you'll limit your ability to contribute to the project or earn kudos for your great results.

If you can't admit mistakes, you won't be able to learn about what's missing or what went wrong in order to improve. Striving to do great work is good for your career, but carried too far, you'll spin and stagnate as you try—fruitlessly—to achieve an unrealistic standard.

Know when enough is enough, and be satisfied with delivering on a project where you've performed well, if not flawlessly. Rather than waiting to release your work until it's perfect, get comfortable with incremental improvement over time and the career benefits of continuous learning.

# HOW TO BE LESS PERFECTIONISTIC

So how might you shift from your perfectionist tendencies? Whether you're a confirmed perfectionist or a personality who is always driving for too much, you can change. Here are some suggestions.

**Change your mind.** The old adage is true: "Change your thinking, change your life." Recognize that you're limiting yourself and seek to think differently—taking the pressure off yourself to be all things to all people all the time. Know you can't possibly do it all, and reassure yourself that whatever you do well is a contribution to the community and to your colleagues. When you realize you can't do everything and can't do it perfectly, you actually liberate yourself to focus. You can choose what you'll prioritize and where you'll invest your energy rather than spreading yourself so thin that you fail to feel good about anything.

**Find a friend.** Change is always easier when you go through it with a buddy. Find a trusted colleague with whom you can compare notes and who can give you feedback and validate your efforts as well as challenge you when you're getting stuck. Check in regularly, and share how things are going. The process of reflecting with a friend and feeling known and understood can help you make progress.

**Be selective.** Another way to manage perfection is by assessing what's most important for your performance and growth.

There may be tasks that are less important or less consequential, and you can put less into those, while other tasks demand a higher level of effort. You'll want to do quality work in everything, but you can be intentional about which elements of your work get the highest levels of exertion.

**Set deadlines**. It is true that work expands to fit available time, so set deadlines for your projects. Give yourself a time frame for your work, and when you hit the limit, call the outcome good enough. Strive to do your best, and be ready to say something is good enough when it's time to complete the task.

**Adopt a mantra.** Sometimes it can be helpful to adopt a saying that will help you stay focused on your goal. Pick something that works for you, and use it to reinforce the new behavior you want to adopt. For example, tell yourself, "Done is better than perfect." Or "Don't confuse excellence with perfection." Keep these in mind as you seek to change your beliefs and your behaviors.

Excellence is certainly linked with career advancement, but perfection is not. For all kinds of reasons, perfection can limit you—in terms of your performance, relationships, well-being, and happiness. No human is perfect, but you can reimagine "perfect" as embracing your imperfections. Be truly you. Own it—your talents and strengths as well as your limitations.

► **REFLECT**

What are the tasks in which you feel more pressure to be perfect?

# Self-Sabotage

You have intentions for happiness and career progress and pursuing excellence over perfection. But you may also find yourself sabotaging your own success or undermining your advancement and missing out on joy and fulfillment.

Unfortunately, obstructing your own progress is more common than you might think, and it's related to depression as well as stress. In fact, 45 percent of people reported they feel stressed, while 36 percent said they felt scared or depressed and 25 percent were demotivated, according to a poll by Clarify Capital.

In addition, 38 to 44 percent experienced feelings of overwork, burnout, underappreciation, and lack of satisfaction or joy, according to data from the Muse. All this is linked to a high prevalence of people who separate themselves from success.

While blocking yourself is related to depression and stress, it's typically driven by anxiety. You worry about the what-ifs—what will happen if you succeed and face increased workload or pressure. Or you may overthink, focusing on worst-case scenarios for your potential future. It is for these reasons that deterring your own improvement is also related to perfectionism.

## ADOPT A GROWTH MINDSET

Interestingly, undermining your success may be related to your thinking patterns. According to one study, when people had a fixed view of success—meaning they believed talent was a stable characteristic rather than something that could be developed continuously—they tended to become especially anxious when they achieved success.

On the other hand, when people had a growth mindset with a more flexible view of their skills and capabilities, they tended to embrace their achievements, according to research at the University of Toronto.

Based on this research, you're smart to remind yourself that your success is the result of hard work, that you can learn continuously, and that development is lifelong.

## EXPRESS YOURSELF

You can also embrace success by expressing yourself effectively. Speak up, communicate with confidence, and own your point of view. Avoid using too many qualifiers when you share your ideas. For example, instead of saying "I think we should establish our project plan," or "Maybe we should change our approach to customers," remove the words *think* and *maybe* to make your point more assertively and drive your credibility.

Another way you may be blocking success is by not owning your accomplishments. When you receive a compliment, just say thank you rather than downplaying your efforts. You don't want to become egotistical, of course, but you can be self-assured without being arrogant.

## MAKE EMPOWERED CHOICES

Another way people tend to undermine their own success is by saying no too often. Popular wisdom about boundaries and work-life advises saying no—a lot. But if you're energized by something and believe it will help you develop, you are wise to go after the opportunity.

Choose smart risks, take initiative, and reach out. Put yourself forward for the promotion, ask someone to mentor you, and request the chance to solve a problem or implement your new idea. All these will send a message about your motivation, but they will also empower you and reinforce your value for yourself.

## WORK WITH OTHERS CONSTRUCTIVELY

One of the ways we understand ourselves is in how we interact with others, and our relationships are a mirror of who we are and what we value. So one of the ways you can ensure you're accepting success is by offering help to others and also by asking for support when you need it.

You block your success if you resist aiding others but also if you avoid asking for help and fail as a result. Both offering help and asking for help will assist you in success, and they'll also contribute toward building strong relationships.

Sometimes anxiety can also lead to controlling or micro-managing behavior. Focus instead on taking the appropriate level of control based on what you're responsible for and giving guidance or input to others. But stop short of looking over people's shoulders or becoming overbearing.

You can also ensure you're not creating unnecessary conflict. Be assertive and express your opinions, but don't undermine your success by making everything a battle or prioritizing dis-agreements over relationships. Ensure when you debate or work through conflict that you're maintaining respect for the people involved and their differing perspectives.

Another classic way people undermine their own success is by withdrawing or avoiding others. Reach out, and be inten-tional about building relationships—even in situations where you may be anxious or uncertain. Building strong networks and collegial trust is a surefire way to succeed but also to sustain more happiness in your work and life.

## MANAGE YOURSELF

Ensuring you're not sabotaging your success is also related to how you manage yourself. Set your goals at challenging but rea-sonable heights. If you set them too high or too low, you'll be getting in your own way. In addition, be kind to yourself, and avoid negative self-talk. Remind yourself of all you've achieved and of how capable and resilient you are. Give attention to what you do well and all the ways you'll develop from here.

In addition, take accountability. If you fail, reflect on how you'll do things differently next time. If you miss the mark, own your mistake, and commit to doing better in the future. Taking responsibility contributes to your own empowerment, self-esteem, and confidence.

Also take action. Procrastination is a classic way you may undermine your success, so set things in motion, and execute on tasks. Even small steps can keep you moving forward in positive ways.

Undermining your own success is a challenge, especially today because there is so much pressure in the world, translating into stress or anxiety in work and life. But you can be intentional about how you embrace your capability and your potential and drive your own happiness, joy, and fulfillment.

▶ REFLECT

Have you ever undermined your own success?

_____

_____

_____

# Imposter Syndrome

Imposter syndrome—the sense that you're not good enough even when you're performing brilliantly—is a dynamic you've certainly heard of before, but new evidence suggests it's even more widespread than previously thought.

It's important to understand imposter syndrome, because it can get in the way of doing your best work, but perhaps more importantly, it can get in the way of your happiness and fulfillment.

## DEFINING IMPOSTER SYNDROME

People with imposter syndrome lack a belief or confidence in their own capabilities or their ability to generate meaningful outcomes. There are two sides to the phenomenon. On the one hand, when those with the syndrome are successful, they attribute it to luck, chance, or external circumstances. On the other hand, when they fail, they internalize the mistakes and believe their shortcomings are impossible to overcome.

In addition, they tend to live in fear of being found out, and they feel like frauds. When others give them positive feedback, they tend to believe the positive perspectives are flawed or provided just for the sake of flattery.

## IMPACTS OF IMPOSTER SYNDROME

The phenomenon can have negative career and personal consequences. When people experience imposter syndrome, they tend to undermine their own performance because they lack confidence and resist owning their success. They may also avoid pursuing new opportunities—especially those that require them to stretch or take professional risks.

Research from Martin Luther University Halle-Wittenberg indicates that a broad array of people experience imposter syndrome. While the syndrome was previously attributed to women or those earlier in their careers, the study found the syndrome is prevalent across genders, ages, and intelligence levels.

The study also found imposter syndrome is not correlated with intelligence or performance. It is truly a misperception that a person has about their own capabilities. In addition, imposter syndrome is correlated with greater incidence of depression.

Of course, some level of reflection, critical thinking, and scrutiny can be healthy for personal and professional growth. Self-awareness helps people identify flaws and work to improve, but imposter syndrome takes healthy self-reflection to an extreme and can leave people drowning in feelings of self-doubt or obsession about mistakes.

# HOW TO COPE

Those with imposter syndrome can take positive action to manage it in a number of ways.

**Surround yourself with people who care.** When you're questioning your own capabilities, it can be especially helpful to spend time with friends who will provide honest feedback and who will remind you of your strengths.

**Balance your time.** Feelings of inadequacy can drive perfectionism, obsessing, or overwork. Be sure to manage your time and your energy, investing where it's appropriate and taking time away to recharge and reset.

**Track your progress.** People tend to magnify negative feedback and minimize positive achievements. To counteract this common cognitive bias, track your progress so you can provide yourself with validation of all you've accomplished and all you've learned along the way.

**Don't wait.** It is a myth that you need to wait for things around you to be ideal in order to be happy—when the project is finished or when the challenging boss moves on to another role for example. Instead, recognize your own ability to create the conditions for joy and happiness. Remind yourself of how you contribute to the community. Connect with people around you, and support others. Foster gratitude, and seek opportunities for new learning. All these are correlated with greater happiness in your work.

Understanding imposter syndrome can help those who experience it to take action, but others can also provide support as well. Tune in to colleagues, ask questions, empathize, and provide recognition and appreciation for those who are doing good work around you. Through these approaches, you'll support those who may question their own capabilities and contribute to an overall positive experience and constructive culture as well as happiness.

▶ REFLECT

In which parts of your life do you feel most confident and capable?

_____

_____

_____

_____

_____

_____

_____

_____

_____

_____

_____

## HAPPINESS IN PRACTICE

- ► Maeve was trying to set up a coffee chat with a friend at work. Her friend said she couldn't imagine how Maeve could find time based on all she had going on and how busy she was. Maeve realized not only how full her calendar was but also the way people perceived her to be racing around all the time. She made a conscious decision to talk less about "how busy" she was when coworkers asked how she was. Instead, she talked about the interesting project she was working on or what she did over the weekend. By changing her language and her focus, she found that she felt less frenetic, but she also found that her relationships became richer, because people perceived she had more time to spend with them and valued them more.

## HAPPINESS IN ACTION

- ► Adopt a playful mindset.
- ► Be forgiving with yourself and others, and remind yourself of your power and capabilities.
- ► Give yourself permission to slow down and reject a too-much, too-fast, always-on mentality.

# 7

# CHOOSING ALTERNATIVES

Sometimes you may find yourself in a job you don't love or bored with your work, but you can thrive anyway. In addition, there may be times when you want to consider leaving your job and renewing your path to happiness.

## How to Thrive in a Job You Don't Love

You know that to grow your career, you must perform with gusto in your current role. That can be tough, however, if it doesn't seem like a great fit or if it doesn't inspire you. Sometimes the path to your next opportunity can be a bit rocky or a bit bland. Either way, a reset may be necessary. Here's how to not only bide your time until your next role but to thrive and choose joy as you strive toward the next career step.

**Make friends.** Find people at work with whom you can build a relationship and whom you appreciate. If your job is especially unpleasant, the people slogging through next to you can be the most important part of your survival. Misery likes company, yes, but even more, people can help pick you up when you're down.

**Focus on the positive.** If you're not loving what you do, focus on small, positive elements. Perhaps the commute is easy or the hours are good. If you don't like the content of your work, maybe at least the company has a constructive culture. Being grateful for (even) small things will do worlds for your attitude and your survival until the next opportunity presents itself.

**Focus on what's next.** While today's work may not be all you hoped it would be, you're always on a path toward what's next. Intentionally set your vision on your next role. Imagine what you will do, how you'll build your skills, and the ways you'll reach out to gain support from mentors. The clearer you are about what's next, the more you can make positive efforts toward that next step.

**Push your patience button.** When our friend's son whines for what he wants, he tells him, "Push your patience button." This is good advice for adults too. Not every job will be rainbows and butterflies, so be patient with where you are. Careers need to grow over time, and *time* can be the operative word. All careers also go through ups and downs. So whether you're developing toward the next step or in a rut on your career journey, be patient. Know things will change—often faster than you think.

**Learn what not to do.** We tend to think the best learning is through positive experiences. But in actuality, some of the deepest learning comes from tough situations. If your boss is a tyrant, focus on what you can learn about your own future approach to leadership—what you'll do differently. If your company doesn't value people or foster a positive culture, focus on what you can learn about what to look for in the best companies. You'll have a list of criteria at the ready when you're seeking your next role. Learning through negative experiences can be as powerful as learning through positive ones.

**Get all you can from the company.** Perhaps you don't love your job but the company offers great benefits. Now may be the time to get that elective surgery or complete your degree using the company's tuition reimbursement program. You're contributing through your good work, so it's fair for you to leverage all the company has to offer in the meantime.

**Focus your extra energy.** If your job isn't stimulating, take advantage of the brain capacity your role doesn't require. Mentally develop that novel you've been wanting to write, or envision the ideal house you'll design and build. Our mental functions can be as stimulating as those in the physical world, so embrace the cognitive opportunities.

Overall, know that a not-so-great job won't last. The leader will change. The company will evolve. And the content of the work will certainly develop. Hang in there, and your positive approach over time will certainly pay off in your next great opportunity, and it will contribute to greater joy in the present.

► **REFLECT**

What have you learned from a job you didn't love?

_____

_____

_____

_____

_____

_____

_____

_____

_____

_____

_____

_____

# When to Leave Your Current Job

Sometimes a job or a company isn't what you had hoped it would be when you signed on, and it's just not the right context for happiness. Of course, it's important to give your best effort toward success, but how do you know when you're just beating your head against the wall and it's time to make a change?

Start by committing to being successful in your current job and company. Build your resilience, and manage your own expectations. Then, if you've done your best and things still don't feel like they're working out, consider these signals that it's time to take advantage of your options and find your next opportunity.

**Your work doesn't matter.** Every job has aspects that are less exciting. But it's time to make a change when you feel like your work doesn't matter. Stay at a job where you have a sense of purpose and connection to the bigger picture and where you feel like you and your work are important to the overall success of the team. Stay in a role where you can take risks and stretch. Stay at a job where you feel stimulated. Not every day has to be exciting and packed with deep meaning, but if you're not getting these opportunities, it's probably time to move on.

**You can't see the next step.** Even if your current job isn't perfect, it's smart to stay with a company where you can see the next step. On the other hand, if the company lacks opportunities for development, training, or mentorship, it might be time to move on. One of the symptoms of burnout is an inability to see future growth opportunities. It's your responsibility to go after new options and make yourself known, but if you can't get anyone's attention in your workplace, you'll want to find a place where you can.

**You're disconnected from your colleagues.** A sense of belonging is critical to our happiness, and we experience social pain in the same parts of the brain where we experience physical pain. If you've tried to connect but still feel excluded or disconnected from your team or your colleagues, you may be in the wrong group. Cultural fit is personal and relative. The best organization for one person may not be the best for another. So just because you look around and see satisfied colleagues, the team may still not be the best fit for you. Consider trying another team or job within the company, and if you still don't feel a sense of comfort and connectedness, make a change.

**You can't be yourself.** This is perhaps one of the biggest factors in knowing when to seek another role or different company. You must be able to be fully yourself to be at your best. Of course, you should apply this idea within reason; even the most wonderful company probably doesn't want you to show up in your jammies or interact with you when you're in your worst mood. But in general, you need a place where you can apply your skills and talents, rock your unique sense of humor, and be appreciated for the idiosyncratic gifts you bring. If you're not valued, or if there is a lack of reward or recognition for your contributions, it's time to consider making a leap.

**You're in a bad environment.** A culture is significantly defined by the worst behavior it tolerates. If there is a lot of bad behavior in your company and people aren't held accountable for it, the environment can become toxic. Pay attention to your organization's heroes. The behavior of those who are lauded and promoted affects the culture. If that's not the kind of behavior you value, take it as an important cue. If your office fails to support your work or leaves you sapped at the end of the day, it may be another signal to leave.

There is one caveat in this discussion: in addition to deciding it's time to leave, you'll also want to consider your vision for what's next and how you'll get there. Rather than just *getting out* of your current situation, you'll also want to *get on* with pursuing a positive vision of your future. This will be important in convincing hiring managers of your value and in keeping yourself energized to take the next step.

Commit, invest, and give a job and a company a fair shot. But trust your instincts when it's time to make a change, and in that case, make the leap toward your best and most joyful future, because you deserve it and because it is critical to your sense of joy.

## ► REFLECT

Have you ever left a job for a better opportunity?

# Boredom

My mom used to call boredom the "b-word," and it was banned in our household. Her problem with boredom was philosophical. If you were bored, it wasn't because there was nothing to do. It was because you hadn't put enough effort into keeping yourself busy.

As always, Mom wasn't wrong.

Being bored has become vogue. New studies point to how boredom is actually good for creativity and innovation as well as mental health. For example, a study published in *Creativity Research Journal* found that people were more creative following the completion of a boring task. Another research effort detailed in *Journal of Experimental Social Psychology* found that when people were bored, they had an increase in "associative thought"—the process of making new connections between ideas linked to innovative thinking. While these studies are impressive, in reality, the "benefits of boredom" may actually be simply having time to clear your mind, be quiet, or daydream.

The truth is *real* boredom isn't pleasant. In fact, one study published in *Science* found that participants (67 percent of men and 25 percent of women) chose to administer an electric shock to themselves rather than sit and think quietly for six to fifteen minutes.

In our stimulation-rich world, it seems unrealistic that boredom could occur at all. Yet there are legitimate reasons boredom may feel so painful. It turns out boredom is a signal of a need that isn't being met.

**Boredom can point to a need for more connections.** Our always-on world of social media may result in more connections, but as I've said, they are superficial and can get in the way of building a real sense of belonging. Feeling bored may signal the desire for a greater sense of community and the feeling that you fit in with others around you. Join a club, organization, or association to build face-to-face relationships and create new friendships—finding depth you won't get from your screen no matter how many likes you get on your post.

**Boredom can point to a need to contribute.** Just as with the need for belonging, people who are bored often report they feel a limited sense of meaning. A fundamental human need is for purpose and to feel we're part of something bigger than ourselves. A University of Mississippi study found that when people are bored, they are more likely to feel less meaning in their lives and vice versa. Conversely, a study at the University of Southampton found that when people volunteered, their happiness increased. To reduce boredom and increase your sense of meaning, seek work that matters to you and for which you can make a unique contribution, or find a cause you can support with your time and talents.

**Boredom can suggest you would benefit from being more challenged.** People have varying needs for stimulation and adrenaline rushes, but in general, boredom may be a signal you need to push yourself a bit. This could be a stretch at work or in your leisure activities. Happiness is correlated with being challenged and developing new skills; scrolling through your social media accounts doesn't meet this requirement. Find opportunities to try new things. Whether it's skydiving, taking on a tough project at work, or starting a hobby that provides a fun outlet, seek these productive antidotes to boredom.

**Boredom may suggest you need more variety.** One of the aspects of boredom is feeling like things are the same day to day and week to week. While some predictability is good for mental health, you may also need more variety in your life. Invite people of different backgrounds into your friend group, join the unexpected interest group at work, or read more widely on unusual topics—anything to broaden your perspective and change what you're exposed to regularly.

**Boredom may signal the need for depth.** Because of the internet and the habits we've established in surfing it, our brains have been rewired to graze the surface of things rather than to go deep. In fact, the ability to have more depth, process deeply, and really get into flow are hallmarks of empathy, connectedness, and happiness. Find the project in which you can lose yourself because it's so interesting, or set aside time to solve a tough problem. These kinds of deep thinking can alleviate boredom as well.

► **REFLECT**

What kinds of activities bore you?

_____

_____

_____

_____

_____

_____

_____

_____

_____

_____

_____

_____

_____

_____

_____

_____

_____

_____

_____

_____

_____

_____

# Learning from Poor Experiences

In addition to being in a job you don't love or being bored, you can also experience deteriorating happiness if you're around people who are rude, negative, or behaving badly.

In fact, misbehavior seems to be on the rise—from air travelers getting into fights to executives throwing temper tantrums. According to research at the University of Chicago, 74 percent of Americans believe manners and civility have deteriorated over the past several decades.

Fortunately, it is possible to find the silver lining when you experience bad behavior and to take your own lessons from it and nurture your happiness despite what might be going on around you. And it's critically important, since a lack of civility at work—things like rudeness, sarcasm, demeaning language, interrupting, or talking over others—can cause high levels of stress and even interrupt sleep, according to a study published in *Occupational Health Science*. A poll by FlexJobs also found that people report increased anxiety (51 percent), mental fatigue (44 percent), and physical challenges (33 percent) as well as problems with depression, engagement, and productivity when they worked with colleagues who demonstrated bad behavior.

While social standards differ from workplace to workplace, there is fascinating research to suggest that many of us are surprisingly aligned about what kinds of behaviors are considered good and which are unacceptable. Anthropologists from the University of Oxford analyzed sixty different societies and found that there are seven universal moral rules: help your family, help your group, be brave and take appropriate risks, demonstrate respect for superiors, divide resources fairly, respect others' property, and return favors (reciprocate).

These rules relate to the workplace. We all want coworkers to be good team players and demonstrate respect for others around them—especially coworkers who may know more or be able to provide guidance. And we all appreciate coworkers who do their fair share and reciprocate in helping others. It's when these deep-seated moral rules aren't followed that we feel the most frustration.

Here are the seven lessons you can learn from even your most difficult coworker.

**Learn how to make an impact.** You can learn from the irritations you have with others and improve yourself over time. One lesson you can learn from dealing with difficult coworkers is how to be a role model for others. We learn by watching, listening to, and experiencing others. How you show up when dealing with a difficult coworker impacts those around you.

In addition, when you do your best in the face of others' bad behavior, you contribute to your own credibility and set yourself apart. Colleagues typically want to work with positive performers, and organizations often reward those who demonstrate commitment and initiative. Ultimately, when you do great work, you also contribute to your own sense of self-esteem. It can be frustrating to be a standout among people who aren't doing their best, but you'll feel better looking in the mirror each morning.

**Learn the importance of doing your fair share.** It can be frustrating when you believe others aren't doing their fair share. The trend of quiet quitting when people do the bare minimum to get by may have even exacerbated this. Unfortunately, when coworkers shirk responsibility, their behavior can put pressure and unfair responsibility on others. A coworker who fails to do their part can behave in many ways. Colleagues who do less than their workload may make excuses in order to avoid taking on a task. They may fail to take initiative. Or they may ask others for help before they've attempted to do something on their own. This can also manifest in people who mess up and then try to hide a problem, creating bigger issues in the long run.

When you are frustrated about these kinds of behaviors, you may be able to learn a lesson in commitment and effort. Do your best, do your part, and put your best work forward. Recognize problems, and take the initiative to solve them. And own your mistakes so that you can get better all the time. Plus, when you're productive and make a strong contribution, you'll be more likely to be happy and fulfilled at work. According to a poll by ClickUp, when people considered themselves to be productive, they were four times more likely to report satisfaction at work.

**Learn how to follow through.** It can also be frustrating when coworkers fail to keep their commitments or say they'll do something and then fail to complete the task. People who aren't willing to take responsibility and accountability drag the team down. People also demonstrate this behavior by overdelegating—getting others to do things they should be doing themselves. Or by poorly managing their time and then asking others for help at the last minute. Or by failing to provide deliverables in time for others to do their portion of a task.

From these examples of bad behavior, you can focus on stepping up, following through, and delivering on your promises. Make commitments to get things done when they're in your lane, and then complete tasks as promised. Exercise empathy in your work by understanding what others are facing and ensuring you're doing your job well so that others can be successful as well.

"Responsibility aversion" is a psychological term that describes when people avoid responsibility because they don't want to take on the emotional costs associated with outcomes or take ownership for others' experience. However, taking responsibility is key to leading any team successfully—whether you're in a position of formal leadership or expressing leadership and influence as an individual contributor. Working with a difficult coworker can teach you how to embrace responsibility and the influence you can have on your team.

**Learn how to be detail oriented.** It's frustrating when colleagues make mistakes continually or do subpar work. Everyone messes up and needs grace and forgiveness, but when issues occur repeatedly, people tend to conclude the coworker just isn't making the necessary investment in their work.

If you experience this, you can reinforce your own orientation for detail. Be sure you show up on time, proofread your work, and check it over to be sure you're not missing things. Deliver great results, whether they are big or small. People often pay the most attention to big responsibilities and tasks, but each small choice you make also sends a message about your priorities, conscientiousness, and care for others.

**Learn how to take feedback.** Another common point of annoyance with difficult coworkers is that they can be defensive when given feedback and are typically unwilling to learn and improve. Difficult coworkers often fail to understand their own mistakes and resist input or guidance about how to improve.

From this experience, you can learn how to take feedback productively. Do your work, reflect on it, and determine how you performed and whether you can improve. Regularly ask for feedback from team members or leaders, and then be open to what they have to say. Ask for help, and seek guidance when you need it. People respect and appreciate when you perform well and when you realize the need for improvement. Being able to incorporate feedback will improve your credibility as a team player and can help you advance in your career.

**Learn how to relate to others.** Annoyance with colleagues can be the result of what they're doing—the content of their work—but also how they interact with others. This can include rudeness, disrespect, bullying, complaining, or failing to consider others' points of view. It could even include interacting poorly with customers. When people relate with others poorly, the behavior can be among the most difficult challenges to overcome. Conversely, good relationships among members tend to positively affect the whole team.

If you are dealing with a coworker who has a hard time interacting with others, focus yourself on intentionally investing in your own relationships and being respectful of others. Conflict is natural in teams, so build your skills in listening, asking questions, seeking to understand, and working through issues directly and constructively. Express opinions, but be open to others' points of view as well. And assume good intentions in others, since doing so affects how you relate and can begin a positive cycle of interacting.

Interestingly, getting to know others can also help productivity. When you can see where someone is coming from and feel empathy toward them, it tends to build relationships and enhance the way people accomplish tasks together.

**Learn how to call out bad behavior.** Perhaps the most valuable lesson you can learn when dealing with a disrespectful coworker is how to stand up for others. The culture of an organization is determined by the worst behavior it will tolerate, and few things are as damaging to a culture as bad behavior that is ignored or allowed. How you show up, communicate, interact, and deliver your work greatly impacts your team.

Don't underestimate your own influence on others. Know that when you're working with people who disappoint, frustrate, or annoy you, you can make different choices that benefit your own self-esteem and outlook as well as those of the people around you.

▶ REFLECT

What is one lesson you've taken away from a bad experience?

_____

_____

_____

_____

_____

_____

_____

# Professional Courage

Professional courage is a skill that gets little mention, but it is critical to career growth, happiness, and fulfillment. It is a fundamental element of leading—whether you're in a formal leadership role or not—and it is critical to your career and personal growth.

Contrary to popular belief, courage isn't the absence of fear. Instead, it is taking action and proceeding forward in spite of fear. Some have said it is when conscience, fear, and action come together. It is grit, perseverance, and determination.

## THE NATURE AND SCIENCE OF COURAGE

Professional courage is a special brand of bravery because it is rarely defined as an impulsive battlefield moment with lifesaving potential. Rather, professional courage involves making bold choices while avoiding career-limiting effects. It involves an ability (or an instinct) to sense opportunities and then suss out the right response and timing.

In addition, professional courage relates significantly to decision-making and to being sensitive to both your own emotions and to the context around you. These sensitivities help you avoid impulsive action and ensure the timing will be right for your response.

Interestingly, we tend to be overly confident about our own courage. A study by Carnegie Mellon University found people tend to overestimate the extent to which they will take action—for themselves or others—when they are faced with a dangerous situation. Actually, courage is built over time through repetition and experience more than through imagination.

Courage is also driven by key regions of the brain. A study by the Weizmann Institute of Science in Rehovot, Israel, found that when people display courage, their frontal and temporal brain regions are most involved. These are the areas responsible for decision-making and for perception and memory.

In moments of courage, we are collecting information, assessing, determining the best reactions, and then cementing the experience into memory for the next moment when courage is necessary.

## BENEFITS OF COURAGE

Courage has plenty of benefits that create the case to develop your determination. First, your own happiness and fulfillment are significantly affected by courage. When you act in alignment with your values, you tend to be happier and more satisfied, so the courage to stand up for what you believe is worth cultivating.

In addition, when you stretch, strive, and seek new experiences outside your comfort zone, you tend to be happier and more fulfilled. The definition of thriving includes elements of success but also elements of continual growth and improvement.

Courage motivates you to reach for more and constantly seek the next best version of yourself, and this contributes to happiness and fulfillment.

Courage also helps you step beyond your comfort zones, and this provides you with greater perspective and expanded experiences that help you succeed in future situations that may be unfamiliar. Having gone through more, you have greater reserves on which to draw. This resilience is especially helpful in the future of work, which will be increasingly ambiguous and fast-moving.

Courage can also enhance your credibility and relationships. People respect and appreciate those who have clear convictions and who take action on them. In addition, when you do the right thing, the positive effects are likely to impact not just you but others around you, and this can build relationships and contribute to the broader community.

It is also worth noting that courage tends to beget courage. When you act with bravery and regularly stand up for others, for your values, or for yourself, you develop your comfort and competence for the next time and the next.

The Finnish concept of *sisu* applies here. Studies at Aalto University found the deeply held cultural construct suggests we can surpass perceived limitations and access storehouses of inner strength. These can get us started on a long journey or keep us going, demonstrating determination. It is the idea of "embodied fortitude"—the demonstration of grit.

## TYPES OF COURAGE

You can demonstrate courage in a variety of ways. Courage always involves choices that affect others and that cause you to move forward or hold back based on your discretion.

**Stand with.** Sometimes, a colleague may need support, and you can express your bravery by standing with them. If a coworker has been wronged, overlooked, or verbally dismissed, it is a great time to stand with them. When a coworker is belittled by a boss in a meeting, you can speak up on her behalf, reinforcing her performance. You can stand with teammates in a constructive way that is also firm and determined.

**Stand up.** You can also demonstrate bravery by being yourself and owning your performance. Be strong in expressing your talents, but also be open in expressing where you don't know it all. Own your mistakes, and seek feedback about how to be better. Keep commitments, follow through, and avoid stalling or procrastinating. Take responsibility when you perform brilliantly but also when you misstep and know you can do better. Accountability requires courage because when you do well, you must be confident enough to feel good about your success, and when you can do better, you must be confident enough to admit the gap and fill it. Being courageous about your own performance allows you to grow.

**Stand for.** Express your courage through your values as well. Do the right thing for yourself but also for others as a member of a community. A study by Ohio State University found when students didn't cheat, they tended to rate higher on measures of courage, empathy, and honesty, and they also tended to have a greater belief in the honesty of others around them. Know what matters most to you, and don't be shy about articulating your views. Do this in a way that others can hear you, and also seek to learn from others. Open yourself to others so you can gain new perspectives and continually develop your own opinions over time. As the saying goes, "When you know better, do better." Start with a strongly held belief, and seek to expand your understanding of different perspectives so you can ensure your responses are as empathetic and holistic as possible.

**Stand down.** Sometimes the most courageous action is to step away or to compromise. True courage includes discerning what matters most and where you'll expend your energy. It is choosing your battles and letting go when they are not as critical. Real courage isn't truculent or reckless—fighting at every turn. It is the ability to pause, consider, and act with discretion. Compromising can be the best of courage. You represent your values or those of your group, listen to others' preferences, and then find creative ways to meet the needs of the whole as much as possible and keep things moving ahead.

**Keep standing.** Courage is also demonstrated over time when you persevere. You may be turned down for the promotion on your first try, and being brave means putting yourself out there again (and again). You may go through multiple rounds of interviews, but grit requires you to keep at it and maintain your confidence and grace. You also demonstrate courage through creativity. If you don't succeed at first, you may need to find a novel way to solve the problem or an innovative solution that surprises the system. A hallmark of courage is to keep at it, even when the process is difficult.

## HOW TO DEMONSTRATE COURAGE

In order to demonstrate courage, you need to know a few things.

**First, know yourself.** Understand your goals and your values so you can decide which actions matter most. Certain career goals may motivate you to take that expat role or reach for the next job that will stretch your current skills. Your values will dictate which issues require your actions. Also know your own emotional responses. If you're going over the cliff of anger, it may be best to pause and consider your next best action.

**Know your limits.** Often growth requires you to go outside your comfort zones and embrace new situations, take new actions, or venture out despite being unsure or afraid. Putting forward a risky idea or recommending a novel approach may require you to go in new directions. Realize how you'll need to stretch so you can be prepared to take forward action.

**Know the situation.** Classic business systems (think: failure mode and effects analysis) require you to assess the likelihood of failure and the potential negative effects. For actions that aren't likely to succeed and that may have potentially damaging effects, you'll want to ensure you have contingency plans in place. Stay informed about potential risks, and know the downsides involved in your choices. Your own awareness is part of your resilience. When you're in the know, you can make sense of things, improvise, and solve problems. Be intentional about your responses. Clarity and smart choices will contribute to your courage but also to your successful outcomes.

**Know your options.** As you're considering responses to situations, ensure you're aware of multiple right answers. If you're in the middle of a debate about how to respond to a customer need, you may be best served to take a forceful approach that ensures your and the company's values are served. If you're seeking to sell an idea at a high-stakes meeting, you may meet with each member of the group one-on-one to garner support before you're in front of the whole group. You can express courage in a frontal approach or in more nuanced strategies, and these will vary based on what's optimal for a particular situation.

**Know others.** Build your social capital in order to build your courage. When you have a strong network of relationships, you can check in and get advice about when to take action and which actions to take. In addition, with a solid network, you will have better support in case you stumble. Doing the right thing for yourself and others repeatedly tends to build your rapport, and this will pay off when you take courageous action that may go against the grain.

Courage is fundamentally optimistic. When you take action in the face of adversity and when you persevere, you're moving forward and contributing to a bright future. You may be making evolutionary change in incremental steps, or you may be making more revolutionary change. Either way, your actions will likely have positive impacts on you but also on the community. Courage is fuel for your success as well as your thriving and happiness.

▶ REFLECT

What is a time you've stood up for yourself or someone else?

--------------------------------------------------------------

--------------------------------------------------------------

--------------------------------------------------------------

## HAPPINESS IN PRACTICE

▶ Jamal had enjoyed his job as a human resources professional for years, but over time, he began feeling less energized by it. He had always loved social justice and decided to take a few classes in that area. Through the networks he built at the local college, he learned about an opportunity working for a nonprofit helping people who were disadvantaged. He left his corporate role and took the new job and hasn't looked back. He says it was especially helpful to follow his interests by taking classes and then being open to the new possibilities that emerged through the people he met in that new circumstance.

## HAPPINESS IN ACTION

▶ Stay hopeful and give your best, as long as it makes sense.
▶ Empower yourself to make alternative choices when it's time to move on from your current role.
▶ Stay motivated. Balance the need for time away with time when you're committing more time and energy to work.

# 8

# CHOOSING MORE

Ironically, your joy at work is partially driven by your life outside work. The way you manage your boundaries will contribute to your happiness, and contrary to having big ambitions, sometimes dreaming small is a better way to capture happiness and meaning in your work. Plus, taking proactive steps and building your resilience will put you on the best path for happiness.

## Creating the Right Boundaries

Have you ever had that pit-in-your-stomach feeling because of a difficult meeting? Or opened your email to see a message that made you close it right down because you knew it would be a tough one? We've all had difficult moments at work, and it would be a rare person who hasn't experienced some of the results of the anxiety they carried home.

Work and life aren't separate, and thus when work isn't perfect, it can intrude on the quality of our lives overall. In general, the perception of spillover from work to family is widespread—across all generations, genders, and varying income levels.

Our experiences at work matter to our lives at work but also to our lives in general. It's impossible to share our best selves with our families, friends, and life partners if we're struggling with high levels of tension at work. But it's possible to create boundaries to protect our lives at home.

**Keep perspective.** First, see the big picture. Work can be challenging, but it doesn't have to be all-consuming. Remind yourself about other things that are important, reassure yourself about all that is positive in your life beyond a particular work issue, and encourage yourself by recognizing what is upsetting today may not even be in your memory a year or two from now.

**Distance yourself.** Create mental separation by consciously putting work aside as you transition to your time away from the office. Finish your call before you enter your home. Lengthen your commute by driving or walking around the block a few times if you need those extra moments to decompress. Even consider taking a shower when you get home—anything to create mental and emotional distance from the source of your work difficulties.

**Make a friend.** It's well known that having a best friend at work contributes to positive work outcomes. But it's also helpful to have a trusted colleague with whom you can obtain perspective and reassurance. In addition, having a coworker you can confide in helps you keep work at work and allows you to be more emotionally available for friends and family at home.

**Be authentic.** It's also important to be open at home when you're challenged at work. Let those who are close to you know you're struggling. Help them understand your difficulties, and let them know that if you're not yourself, it's not about them. But don't dwell. Be ready to move on and focus on what is meaningful to you outside work.

**Focus on others.** Another way to mitigate difficulties is to help others and broaden the focus from yourself to those around you. Challenging situations tend to narrow our views, and we become consumed by our own worries. Volunteering, sharing talents with others, or assisting those in need all have the effect of reducing how we experience our own tension because we're more focused on others.

**Be a beacon.** Never underestimate your own effect on others. Demonstrate caring through your behavior at work, and do your best to avoid being someone else's stressor. Sociologically, our behavior is significantly influenced by the behavior of those around us, so we all have the power and opportunity to have a positive impact on those around us.

▶ **REFLECT**

In what ways do you set boundaries?

_____

_____

_____

_____

_____

_____

_____

_____

_____

_____

_____

_____

_____

_____

_____

_____

_____

# Creating Joy through Dreaming Small

Big dreams and idealistic goals have become the stuff of legend. We laud the woman who has done it all by the time she is in her late twenties, and we idolize the man who has solved world problems over his storied career—and we should. These are great accomplishments, and they can motivate the rest of us.

But I also think a dose of reality is a good thing.

The problem is when we overvalue extreme success, we tend to undervalue ordinary contributions. As I've said before, all work has dignity, and even ordinary good work is valuable. Every positive action is a small contribution toward changing the world in constructive ways. Having realistic goals—rather than over-reaching goals—can even contribute to our sense of well-being.

So how do we value ourselves adequately when the world looks for superheroes and we are mere mortals?

**Reduce the pressure.** Sometimes, when people ask us how we want to make our mark on the world, it doesn't feel motivational; it feels like pressure. We can take the pressure off ourselves and just do good ordinary work. The extraordinary is often just the accumulation of the ordinary. As the popular wisdom suggests, one of the primary secrets of success is showing up.

**Take the next step.** Think small about your efforts. You don't need a path mapped out toward world domination. Just do things to the best of your ability, and do what makes sense next. In the movie *The Martian*, the main character just solves one problem and then the next and the next. Through persistent effort in dealing with each individual trial, he is able to conquer the most extreme challenge in the end.

**Be kind.** You may not be able to accomplish world peace, but by being kind to colleagues and coworkers, you can have a positive impact on those around you. Being kind also results in positive outcomes for ourselves, from optimistic feelings to a better chemical balance of the heart. It seems simple, and it is— but in a really important way.

**Never underestimate your impact.** All this talk about thinking small is actually very big, because we each have an impact on those around us. Our loci of control and influence may be small, but each person we come into contact with also comes into contact with others in their own networks. This is the butterfly effect, based on chaos theory, which posits that small actions can have big impacts. The small and the ordinary can be magnified over time and through our connections with others.

► REFLECT

In what ways do you have an impact on others?

_____

_____

_____

# Meaningful Work

Of course, on the way to finding joy, we may be seeking meaningful work—work that is valuable and has significance. Unfortunately, there is no such thing. It's not there for the taking, and it doesn't exist somewhere for you to simply pluck.

This is both fortunate and unfortunate.

Because like joy, meaningful work is ours to create. This is liberating and empowering. It's also a lot of responsibility. In addition, this is "agency"—the concept that we are actors in our own narratives with the power to develop and adjust our own storylines.

Companies and leaders have some responsibility to help align your talents and your work, but the main responsibility for meaningful work is your own. Here's how to create it for yourself.

**Change your perspective.** Understand that meaningful work is relative and personal. Don't choose work based just on status. Do what you like most. If all your friends are going into office jobs but you love to work with your hands, enter the skilled trades. If everyone you know seems to be going into business but you are motivated by nurturing people, join a helping profession. Also, know that your definitions and experiences may change. What you loved a few years ago may shift, and you should too.

**Find your passion.** While "finding your passion" can feel like a lot of pressure, it doesn't have to. Simply identify things you like to do and that you're good at (and that others value enough so you can cover rent and groceries). There may be things about which you feel overwhelming intensity and a compulsion to pursue. If that's the case, great. If not, find the next right thing, and follow that path.

**Connect with people.** A big part of meaningful work is our connections with others. Go toward opportunities where there are communities of people you enjoy and from whom you can learn. Wonderful work with a group where you feel like an outsider or where you're not supported isn't so wonderful after all. Ensure your work embeds you in places where the people are those you want to be with and with whom you can grow and belong.

**Ensure your purpose is clear.** Connect with your purpose by linking your work to a bigger picture. If you make hardware on an assembly line, consider the mechanism that hardware goes into, the crank it powers, the hospital bed it fits onto, and the way it allows critically ill patients to be moved regularly so their sores heal and they can go home sooner. If you sit at your desk filling out spreadsheets all day, consider the way your work contributes to a social need or good. It's great to be all in for the corporate mission of 15 percent yearly growth, but beyond that, consider how your work ultimately affects the community.

When you find or create meaning in your work, you'll know it. With meaning, you'll feel like *your work has value*. You'll feel like *you're adding value,* and perhaps most important, you'll be reminded *you have value.*

Creating meaningful work for ourselves is vitally important, not just so we can feel good when we're getting out of bed in the morning bleary-eyed and finding our way to our first cup of tea but also so that we can add something to world. Meaning isn't something we can grab, but it is something we can create, and that's great news for cultivating and choosing joy as well.

▶ **REFLECT**

In what ways is your work most meaningful?

# The Joy of Being Proactive

As you're nurturing greater happiness and satisfaction in life and work, another trait to nurture is the ability to be proactive.

Challenges are seemingly everywhere: the job market is tough, stress is rampant, loneliness is epidemic, and people are polarized. But amid all the troubles, being proactive may help.

It's not a panacea (nothing is), but research on being proactive provides powerful evidence that it can help you build your career, contribute to your success, foster positive relationships, nurture your fulfillment, and even make more money.

## PROACTIVE PERSONALITY

Being proactive has actually been found as a unique aspect of personality, according to research published in *Journal of Human Performance*. When people are proactive, they take initiative to influence their environments and embrace personal agency. They are curious and confident, and they seek positive control. They make changes, take action, and avoid passive acceptance of their circumstances, according to research in *Journal of Vocational Behavior*.

It can be helpful to understand what proactive personality is not. According to research published in *Psychology Today*, being proactive is not the same as just being busy or productive, nor is it focused on taking risks. Of course, these can be characteristics of taking action, but being proactive isn't just being busy, adventurous, or audacious—it is being reflective, discerning, and strategic about the action you take.

## PLENTY OF BENEFITS

When people are proactive, they tend to thrive at work and be more satisfied with their careers because they take action across their career stages and therefore experience more growth in their careers, according to *Journal of Vocational Behavior* research. In addition, people who are more proactive tend to benefit by being promoted to leadership roles and making more money, based on research published in the *Journal of Applied Psychology*.

When employees are more proactive, business outcomes are improved through greater effectiveness and enhanced competitiveness. People who take charge, seek feedback, and build strong social networks in turn improve creativity and processes within organizations, according to research published in *Frontiers in Psychology*.

Employees with a proactive bent also help organizations face uncertainty in a challenging business climate, according to research in *Journal of Applied Psychology*.

## HOW TO BE MORE PROACTIVE

Interestingly, research published in *Journal of Applied Psychology* also reports that 40 percent of the tendency to be proactive can be attributed to your genes, but fully 60 percent is based on environmental factors, so it's worth the effort to develop the capability.

**Tune in.** One of the first ways to be more proactive is to tune in, pay attention, and explore your situation. Seek information from sources you know, and explore terrain that may be less familiar to you. Subscribe to the news outlet or journal with new perspectives or opinions that don't match your own. Challenge yourself to stay in touch with what's going on in the world, in your area, at work, and in your community. With high levels of awareness about context, you can be ready to consider the best strategy to move forward.

**Make plans.** Another way to demonstrate proactivity is to look ahead. According to research in *Journal of Applied Psychology*, making long-term plans is characteristic of those who are effectively proactive. Be intentional about where you want to be and what you want to achieve, and set goals accordingly. Try a "backward from perfect" strategy. Aspire for the long term and your ideal, and then work backward to establish the steps that will get you to the end goal you seek.

**Take action.** This is perhaps the most quintessential of proactive behaviors. In addition to checking the context and making plans, you'll also want to take ownership and dive in. When you see problems, take initiative to recommend solutions. When you have responsibilities, follow through and complete tasks. Seek new learning, and explore new career directions, and then take a class or build a relationship with a mentor who can help you grow. Offer to contribute on a project that is related to the career you want to develop, and take on responsibilities that interest you and where you can add value. All these will help you craft your job today and your runway to what will come next.

**Persevere.** Another key element of being proactive is persevering despite obstacles and barriers. Stick with things, even when they're challenging. Demonstrate grit and resilience as you push through. Also be willing to change course when you must. If things don't go as planned, reflect, learn, and adjust for the next time.

**Seek great leaders.** Research in *Frontiers in Psychology* also shows that leaders have a bearing on your ability to be proactive. Seek out leaders who give you opportunities to expand your role, allow you to influence how you get things done, and empower you to make decisions. These help build your confidence and competence. If your direct leader doesn't provide this kind of autonomy or empowerment, look for mentors or coaches who do and assess these traits in the leader for the job you choose next.

Overall, being proactive is something you can embrace, pursue, and develop. Be intentional about how you take action and make things happen.

The mantra is true that to accept the things you cannot change will contribute to your peace of mind. But it's also true there is a lot you can impact, and you have more influence over yourself, your circumstances, and others than you may realize. So commit to building your skills in building your future, and you'll achieve payoffs in your happiness and satisfaction with work and life.

► **REFLECT**

In what ways have you taken action to effect change?

_____

_____

_____

_____

_____

_____

_____

_____

_____

_____

_____

_____

_____

# Building Your Resilience for the Times Ahead

As you move forward, there will rarely be a time with an absence of challenges. The key to survival—and happiness—will be in building your resilience and finding ways to persist and persevere.

Resilience is made up of three things. First, resilience requires a clear sense of reality. Next, it requires the ability to make sense of what's going on. And perhaps most importantly, it requires problem-solving and improvisation. The good news is you can develop all these and become increasingly resilient. Here are a few strategies to help you develop the mental strength.

## KNOW WHAT'S REAL

It's impossible to respond appropriately if you don't have a clear sense of what's going on around you. While it may be tempting to avoid all the bad news, you'll be better served by being aware of the realities around you. Uncertainty and ambiguity are stressful, and knowledge can reduce anxieties around unknown factors.

You don't need to overwhelm yourself with a constant influx of negative content. You can, however, find ways to stay informed. Pay attention to reputable sources of information, and ensure you have a sense of what's new information. Stay in the loop enough to understand context and what's going on around you.

## MAKE SENSE OF THINGS

A big part of being resilient is being able to find meaning in current circumstances. You can do this in a few ways.

**Consider what the current reality means to you.** View conditions with your own lens of what's most important to you.

**Maintain perspective.** It can be tempting to spiral into anxiety about an uncertain future, but try to stay focused on what you can control, and reassure yourself this time will pass. It may be a marathon when we were hoping for a sprint, but you'll get through it.

**Explore new viewpoints.** Seek out multiple perspectives to find meaning in the difficult realities you face. Speak with others, and obtain a variety of points of input. In addition, stay in close touch with people you trust and respect. Your opinions may differ, and it's helpful to expand your thinking and extend your perspectives by exposing yourself to diverse ideas.

## CHALLENGE YOURSELF TO ADAPT

Once you understand reality and have perspective on it, you'll need to respond and adapt. You can do this by solving problems around you and approaching challenges in new ways.

Build your ability to respond by taking on new things that challenge you. Learn a new technical skill, take up a new hobby, or try skydiving. Develop your ingenuity by reaching for professional opportunities as well. Volunteer for a task force, join a team leading the latest work initiative, or start an affinity group. All kinds of new steps or novel stretches are positive ways to build the critical abilities of adapting, responding, and adjusting.

As you move forward, resilience will be one of the most important characteristics to nurture. Be aware, make sense of what's around you, and keep perspective. And most importantly, respond, adapt, and challenge yourself to stretch. With time, you'll develop yourself and have a positive influence on the challenges you encounter.

▸ REFLECT

In what ways have you built your resilience through challenges?

## HAPPINESS IN PRACTICE

▶ Noah had been through a lot. His job was eliminated by his company because of its financial challenges at the same time that his family was going through an especially tough situation. But Noah found a role in a new company, and he was able to begin accomplishing results and receiving positive feedback from his colleagues and his boss. He decided to volunteer within his community, offering career coaching to high school students. He bolstered his happiness by moving through his difficulties and sharing what he'd learned with others.

## HAPPINESS IN ACTION

▶ Set limits and ensure that the distance from work is right for you.
▶ Take action and seek to learn constantly, adjusting as necessary.
▶ Find the extraordinary meaning in your ordinary contributions.

# CONCLUSION

Joy and a deep sense of happiness are yours for the taking. Far from being something you must wait for or something that may be achieved only by a few lucky people, joy is something you can embrace, and happiness is something you can accomplish. Be intentional.

Realize the importance of joy, and don't let myths of work-life balance get in your way or weigh you down.

Keep perspective, be mindful, be optimistic, and realize you can cultivate joyful experiences.

Be selective about the company you choose and the job that most aligns with your passions.

Recognize the impact of social media, and leverage it without letting it control you. Embrace the power of empathy in building relationships, and balance your time working with others and working alone.

Seek opportunities to stretch and say yes more than you say no. Learn from failure, leverage stress, and know that growth and learning contribute to your joy.

Find ways to play and to reject hustle culture. Know when to disconnect and when to pursue your goals with fervor.

Find ways to thrive in a job you don't love, and make tough choices to leave a job that isn't the best fit. Recognize when boredom might be cuing you that it's time to do something different.

Finally, create boundaries, and dream small as you make your work as meaningful as it can be.

Joy is within your grasp. You can create it, cultivate it, and choose it. Enjoy!

# ACKNOWLEDGMENTS

Thanks to my family. I love you immeasurably and appreciate your support, encouragement, ideas, wisdom, coaching, and humor. You are my joy.

Many thanks to my agent, John Willig, and my editor, Meg Gibbons, two of the most positive and encouraging people with whom I've worked. And thanks to the whole Sourcebooks team for their professionalism and expertise in making this book a reality.

To amazing leaders, teammates, mentors, and friends with whom I've worked, thank you for encouraging me, cheering me on, and letting me know when I could do better. Thanks to Rich Isphording for your empowering leadership and to Rebecca Charbauski for your invaluable feedback on my articles.

# ABOUT THE AUTHOR

Dr. Tracy Brower is a PhD sociologist, author, speaker, and thought leader focusing on fulfillment, meaning, and vitality in work and life. Her optimistic voice, refreshing perspectives, and inspirational outlook regularly earn her accolades and awards. Tracy shares her ideas and insights as a contributor to *Forbes*, *Newsweek*, and *Fast Company* as well as many other publications and podcasts. In addition to writing *The Secrets of Happiness at Work*, Tracy is also the author of *Bring Work to Life by Bringing Life to Work: A Guide for Leaders and Organizations*. Her work has been translated into nineteen languages. In addition, she is a vice president of workplace insights with the Applied Research + Consulting group at Steelcase Inc.

Recognized for both her passion and pragmatism, Tracy has

over twenty-five years of experience working with global clients to achieve business results. She is on the board of the United Way and is a coach and executive advisor with the Center for Leadership at Hope College as well as an executive advisor to the Michigan State University Master of Industrial Mathematics program and to the Design Museum Everywhere. Tracy holds a PhD in sociology, a master of management in organizational culture, and a master of corporate real estate with a workplace specialization.

Tracy's work has been featured in TEDx, the *Wall Street Journal, Work-Life Balance in the 21st Century,* Fortune.com, *Inc.,* and *HBR France.* Her work has also received global recognition in publications such as the *Globe and Mail* (Canada), *Inside HR* (Australia), *Director* (UK), *HR Agenda* (Japan), and *t3n* (Germany) as well as conference keynotes in the United States, India, and Asia.

Outside work, Tracy can be found reading, skydiving, and walking marathons (yes, walking them), but she finds her greatest joy spending time with her husband, Terry, their son, Dylan, their daughter and son-in-law, Alexa and Charlie, and their dog, Truffle.

You can find Tracy at tracybrower.com, LinkedIn, or any of the usual social channels.